REDEEMING
your
BLOODLINE

FOUNDATIONS FOR
BREAKING GENERATIONAL CURSES
FROM THE COURTS OF HEAVEN

HRVOJE SIROVINA
& ROBERT HENDERSON

DESTINY IMAGE® PUBLISHERS, INC.
P.O. Box 310, Shippensburg, PA 17257-0310
"Promoting Inspired Lives."

This book and all other Destiny Image and Destiny Image Fiction books are available at Christian bookstores and distributors worldwide.

Cover design by Eileen Rockwell
Interior design by Susan Ramundo

For more information on foreign distributors, call 717-532-3040.
Reach us on the Internet: www.destinyimage.com.

ISBN 13 TP: 978-0-7684-4888-7
ISBN 13 eBook: 978-0-7684-4889-4
ISBN 13 HC: 978-0-7684-4891-7
ISBN 13 LP: 978-0-7684-4890-0

For Worldwide Distribution, Printed in the U.S.A.
6 7 8 / 23 22 21 20

CONTENTS

———•———

INTRODUCTION

This book has been on my heart for a while because I am convinced that it can carry a solution for many who may have longed for breakthrough for a long time. Praying their bloodlines will release many into truly living the life they have been called to. We have received many testimonies during the last decade that confirm this conviction. Yet my greatest joy in all of this is to see King Jesus glorified through all these testimonies.

Although we understand that God does not want to deny anything to His children, we meet people all over the world who love Jesus, yet they do not experience many of God's promised blessings. Jesus has set us free to live a life full of peace, joy, confidence, fun, happiness, overcoming strength, and so much more. The goal of bloodline prayer is to help release people into this liberated and joyful way of life.

While this book is mainly dedicated to the subject of bloodline prayer, it is important to me to clarify that this theme only covers a *part* of our relationship with God. It is significant that our relationship with Jesus is stress-free and founded in joy. He cares about every area of our lives and wishes to participate in every part of it. God wants to share His love, greatness, grace, mercy, confidence, and His plans with us. He also takes interest in the things that bring pleasure to us. He is interested in what we enjoy, but also in what weighs us down. Our heavenly Father is God who desires to take care of us. Jesus is God who never leaves us nor forsakes us. The Holy Spirit is God who helps and counsels us as well as the one who strengthens and elevates us.

Whenever deliverance and bloodline prayer are anchored in this way of life, they are a wonderful process that we can joyfully initiate. It is a process that we expectantly and confidentially walk through. Liberation through bloodline prayer leads us to the foundation of our faith, which is a passionate relationship with God. It is also the crown of our faith and walk with Him.

The teaching and revelation in this book may be new to many. When starting to teach about bloodline prayer, my primary foundation is biblical truth about it. My second foundation is the multiple experiences that we have had in over a decade of this kind of prayer. We had the privilege of learning many things by being active in the courts of heaven, and we would like to share this strategy with many others now.

It is my personal conviction that those revelations will bring forth great breakthroughs that many may have long been waiting for.

So let me tell you about this book now. It contains two parts.

In the first part, I lay a general biblical foundation of bloodline prayer and explain the meaning of the terminology. Please note that the term *bloodline prayer* does not occur in the Bible. It was chosen by us in order to bring revelation about a spiritual, biblical concept. It is interesting that this terminology has been used by Christians every now and then. We had friends in South Africa whose foundation of ministry is in bloodline prayer. I have heard Jimmy Swaggart using it in one of his recorded meetings from 1984. There are many more in the last century. But I haven't found a sound biblical teaching about it, which is why I desire to provide it with this book.

Choosing new terms to express spiritual truths and principles has been a practice throughout church history. This new word or term is simply meant to be a helpful tool supporting the understanding of a vital spiritual concept.

The word *trinity* may be one of the most often used expressions for the triune God. Yet you cannot find it anywhere in the Bible. Nevertheless, it has been used since the second century by church fathers such as Justyn, Irenaeus, Athenagoras, and Tertullian. The term describes the fact that within the one Being who is God, there exists eternally three coequal and coeternal persons—namely, the Father, the Son, and the Holy Spirit.

We use the terminology of bloodline prayer for the very same reason—to help capture a biblical concept.

The second part of this book focuses on the practical application of this principle and consists of prayers we use to lead the reader or the praying person through different areas of repentance. This mainly happens by renouncing covenants that have legal rights in our lives. Legal claims that prevent us from getting our breakthrough, which Jesus has already paid the price for on the cross on our behalf. By bloodline prayer, we dissolve covenants and claims that existed since Adam and that influence our lives.

Please note that this book is not primarily a prayer book to break curses. It is a workbook that helps you to bring redemption for your bloodline. It will enable you to step into the freedom and authority that the Gospel promises us. Seeing curses dissolved is a tremendous byproduct of this kind of prayer. The focus, however, is not breaking those curses but emerging into those new areas of freedom and authority that are required to spread the Kingdom of God in a way it has never been done before.

We pray that your life will be flooded with God's love, blessings, and favor and that its abundance will exceed all your expectations.

In HIS love, Hrvoje Sirovina

PART 1

BIBLICAL FOUNDATIONS
OF BLOODLINE PRAYER

CHAPTER 1

PRAYING ALL THE WAY BACK TO ADAM: WHY?

There are certain disorders in people's lives that can be traced way back to the first man, Adam. Because the effects of his choice not only influenced his own life, but also the lives of his descendants. Because we belong to his posterity, we also have to live with the negative consequences of his actions.

Do we therefore have to accept and put up with them? The very clear answer is no! Paul shows us that Jesus Christ is the solution.

For as in Adam all die, even so in Christ all shall be made alive (1 Corinthians 15:22).

Praying bloodline prayers is one way to actively apply the power of the cross.

The Bible speaks about curses affecting the third and fourth generation (see Num. 14:18). Yet when we pray our bloodlines we pray all the way back to Adam. Now some may ask the question: Why should we pray all the way back to Adam? And this question is certainly justified. The revelation about breaking curses has been spread by the Holy Spirit mainly during the last century. Nevertheless, we must understand that there are curses and bondages that reach further back than the third and fourth generation. The revelation about dissolving curses should not prevent us from receiving even deeper revelation about it and applying it.

Romans 5:14 shows us that there are curses with negative consequences that go way further than the third or fourth generation.

Nevertheless death reigned from Adam to Moses, even over those who had not sinned according to the likeness of the transgression of Adam, who is a type of Him who was to come (Romans 5:14).

Here we see that death reigned over Adam all the way up to Moses and over all mankind. Moses lived 26 generations after Adam. Therefore, Adam's choice had effects on a minimum of 26 generations after him. In this case, death does not speak about a person dying physically. It describes the effects of a covenant that man entered and that excluded God. Not only was this decision a curse that influenced the children and their children's children. No, it was a covenant that was firmly established and would restrict 26 following generations.

There is another question people frequently ask: "Why do we have to pray bloodlines when Jesus has accomplished everything already? Why do we have to break curses or renounce covenants when everything has been done at the cross?" Asking this question is comprehensible and justified. It is this theme I want to expand on to establish the teachings in this book.

The moment we decide that Jesus is our Lord and God, confess Him with our mouth and believe Him in our hearts, righteousness and salvation are granted to us.

However, there are things that do not manifest right away for us through salvation. They are the result of the process of our walk with God. This is commonly referred to as the doctrine of sanctification. Although we are in right standing with God because of the finished work of the cross, we are called to appropriate the power and grace of God to walk out lives of righteousness.

If we study salvation on a deeper level and in a more theological way and do research on what the Bible has to say about it, we should pay special attention to the tenses being used for the doctrine of salvation.

We find Scriptures like Titus 3:5, where the Bible clearly says that we *were saved* (past tense) by God's mercy. This Bible verse clearly speaks about a fact that happened and has been completed in the past.

Yet we read in First Corinthians 1:18 that we *are being saved* (present progressive tense) through the preaching of the cross. So here salvation is described as a process that continuously happens.

The Bible also speaks about another salvation that undeniably is going to take place in the future. It is described in First Peter 1:5, where it is called a "salvation ready to be revealed in the last time."

This is very important to see because it helps as a starting point in order to navigate through the huge number of opinions regarding salvation, grace, and works.

For further examination, let's look at two verses from the first Book of John.

If we say that we have no sin, we deceive ourselves, and the truth is not in us (1 John 1:8).

Whoever has been born of God does not sin, for His seed remains in him; and he cannot sin (1 John 3:9).

One and the same author writes these verses in one and the same book. Reading it might cause us to think that there is a contradiction. But actually these Scriptures help us to understand salvation and why the Bible uses different tenses to describe it.

John says if somebody is born of God he cannot sin. And we know that through salvation we became children of God, which means we are born of God. Yet he also says that we all still sin, and if we deny it we are deceiving ourselves.

In context, when John refers to those who "cannot sin," the sin he describes is persistent, unrepentant sin. He is describing a person who perhaps claims salvation by grace, but who is not benefitting from that grace, and thus, applying it to his or her life. Furthermore, if we are truly born of God (saved), our spirit, redeemed and regenerated by the Holy Spirit, cannot sin because that spirit is under the influence of the Holy Spirit. Let's explore this further to give you context, as this book is not necessarily addressing issues that relate to your eternal destination; rather, issues in the bloodline are aimed at your earthly destiny. Many people will go to Heaven, spiritually, when they die, but these same people will struggle during their time on Earth because of the bloodline issues I am addressing in this book.

How do we bring these Scriptures together without them contradicting each other? Why do we still sin even though the Bible says that everyone born of God can't sin? Understanding this concept and revelation could bring a lot of clarity to all kinds of opinions.

Let me try to explain it this way: The day we receive Jesus into our hearts, our spirit is revived and born of God. Yet there are still two parts of us that need salvation—our soul and our body. Jesus said that our spirit is willing, but our body is weak. Paul describes in Romans 7:21-24 how his inward man, his spirit, delights in the law of God, but there is another law in his members, which is the law of sin. He goes on to describe that he does things he doesn't want to do and that he doesn't do things he wants to do.

You see, even though Paul was clearly saved, yet he still needed salvation in other areas of his being—like we do, too.

The moment we receive Jesus into our hearts, our spirit is revived and of God. I believe from that moment on our spirit cannot sin anymore and constantly battles the sin in our flesh. But our soul and our body still need salvation. I believe the process of continuously being saved is in the part called *soul*—our thoughts, emotions, and will. Even though we have the mind of Christ, we still need our minds being renewed. The salvation that is going to happen in the future is the salvation of our bodies.

Now may the God of peace Himself sanctify you completely; and may your whole spirit, soul, and body be preserved blameless at the coming of our Lord Jesus Christ (1 Thessalonians 5:23).

God wants our whole being to be sanctified, purified, and saved!

The day we were born again our spirit was saved. Yet our soul is constantly being sanctified—being saved, transformed, and conformed to look more and more like Jesus. Our bodies are being cleansed to the point when they will be saved and preserved blameless unto the coming of our Lord Jesus Christ.

As born-again Christians, we are composed of our spirit, soul, and body and we have to take care of all of them. Bloodline prayer is about cleansing what is recorded in our flesh and the nature of our soul.

It is very important to understand that we have to take care of all parts of our being and keep them in check and balance. Even though we live in the earth with our bodies, the Bible says that at the same time we are seated with Christ in heavenly places; this is where our spirit is. But we also often experience that the soul can be at a complete different place at the same time, like David's soul was. In Psalms 86:13, we see that David's soul was captured in Sheol. Too many Christians are saved and seated in heavenly places but are emotionally a wreck. It is because the soul is still captured in Sheol and not every part of their being is positioned at the right place.

The conclusion is our spirit is saved and born of God. Our soul is being saved and sanctified for God. Our flesh is going to be saved and is in the process of cleansing.

Let's take holiness as an example. We do not automatically live in holiness in every area of our life right after our salvation. Holiness is a process, a transformation. Paul says to the believers in Thessaloniki that their sanctification is the will of God for them (see 1 Thess. 4:3). The Greek word *hagiasmos* that has been translated "holiness" defines a process that we need to walk through to become holy.

The same applies to us having the mind of Christ. The Bible says in First Corinthians 2:16 that we have the mind of Christ. Even though Jesus has obtained it at the cross for us, Romans 12:2 tells us that it requires a process of renewal to acquire this new mind.

We therefore see that Jesus has already done everything on the cross and nothing needs to be added to it. Nevertheless, we also see that some things Jesus did require going through a process before they can come into effect.

The righteousness we have through Jesus Christ is our status in God. It empowers us to sanctify our lives.

Often those biblical promises that have an immediate effect on us at salvation are getting mixed up with those promises that require walking with God. It is very important to understand that there are major differences.

INCREASING IN AUTHORITY IS A PROCESS

Authority is one of our favorite subjects to teach about. Particularly because there is significant confusion regarding this subject in the Body of Christ. Biblical clarity and truth are fundamental pillars if we want to see change and breakthrough. For example, it is important to understand that there are different areas of authority—authority over yourself, authority over finances, authority over demons, authority over sickness and disease, authority over regions or nations, and authority to overthrow the strong man of a nation.

Therefore He said: "A certain nobleman went into a far country to receive for himself a kingdom and to return. So he called ten of his servants, delivered to them ten minas, and said to them, 'Do business till I come.' But his citizens hated him, and sent a delegation after him, saying, 'We will not have this man to reign over us.'

"And so it was that when he returned, having received the kingdom, he then commanded these servants, to whom he had given the money, to be called to him, that he might know how much every man had gained by trading. Then came the first, saying, 'Master, your mina has earned ten minas.' And he said to him, 'Well done, good servant; because you were faithful in a very little, have authority over ten cities.' And the second came, saying, 'Master, your mina has earned five minas.' Likewise he said to him, 'You also be over five cities'" (Luke 19:12-19).

The parable Jesus uses here is a perfect picture of how to attain authority in the Kingdom of God.

We see here ten servants received one mina each. Each of the servants received a certain measure of authority—the authority over one mina. This was the realm of authority that was entrusted to them simply because they were servants in the house of their master. The same applies to us. Simply due to the fact that we are children of God and cohabitants in the house of God, we have authority and administration over certain areas.

Now let's have a closer look at this parable: Later the master returned and asked what each servant had done with that mina. The first came to him and returned ten minas to him. Immediately the master increased the realm of authority of this servant. He said that he had been a good administrator and a good steward in his dimension of authority. Therefore, his realm of authority would now increase. He then received authority over ten cities! Please note that he did not have the authority over these cities from the beginning. They were a result of his faithfulness, his administration, and his commitment.

This servant could have declared Philippians 4:13 about himself for years: "I can do all things through Christ who strengthens me," thinking and believing it would give him authority over his city. However, he would have misled himself, because he clearly did not have that authority yet. True authority over cities, regions, and nations is not gained by salvation; it is a result of faithful stewardship. God observes what we do with the realm of authority that has been assigned to us. We only receive more authority if we handle our given authority well. Increasing in authority clearly is a process!

Jesus saying in Mark 9:23 that "All things are possible to him who believes" does not mean that we are immediately capable of doing everything only because we believe it. It means we can acquire all things the Gospel calls us to do. This does not exclude going through the necessary processes, but it encourages us to walk the required distance.

Psalms 119:160 says that the sum of the Word of God is the truth. We need to know and understand the Word of God in its fullness to access more areas of truth and understanding. We cannot retrieve and single out individual Scriptures and more or less ignore the rest. Because the sum, the total computation of His Word is the key for breakthroughs of all kinds. We need to apply biblical processes to receive an increasing measure of authority. We have the confidence and promises that assure us that we will reach our goal by many encouraging Scriptures.

We see from these examples that we must walk through a process of growth to step into the fullness of our promises.

SIN IS STILL ACTIVE INSIDE ME

For what I am doing, I do not understand. For what I will to do, that I do not practice; but what I hate, that I do (Romans 7:15).

This is a very interesting statement by Paul that appears to be a contradiction.

This declaration comes from a tremendously powerful and remarkable apostle. Paul is the apostle who had an amazing encounter with the Lord Jesus Christ. Paul's conversion experience is gigantic. He says that he considers everything else as dirt to gain more of Christ. Paul promotes holiness; endures beatings, shipwreck, and rejection; and he finishes his race getting crowned. What a man!

And this outstanding man says that there are areas in his life where he does things he does not want to do. He even goes a step further and says in verse 17 that these things are done by the sin that dwells on the inside of him.

What exactly does Paul mean when he says that? With this question we have arrived at that place where bloodline prayer is required. It is for areas in our lives about which you could say we have "inherited" them. It is about covenants, contracts, and iniquity that have been handed down to us by our forefathers. Covenants, contracts, and iniquity that have the power to hinder us naturally and spiritually despite our salvation. They prevent us from overcoming and from spreading the Kingdom of God around us.

There is iniquity and there are covenants in our bloodlines that go beyond our immediate forefathers all the way back to Adam. They prevent us from fulfilling our God-given passion.

These claims from previous transgressions go far beyond the Third Reich and Nazi Germany we Germans are so aware of. Those claims go beyond the guilt of the social-communist Soviet Union or China. They go further back than freemasonry; the Germanic people; the Celts, druids, or Aztecs; or the destruction of the Native Americans in North America and beyond.

They go all the way back to Adam. Therefore, it is important that we resolve those covenants going all the way back to Adam! You may think, "No, this is not possible. Jesus has delivered us from all of that." And that is true. But there are areas in our lives in which the completed work of Christ is not immediately made manifest through our salvation. Everything Jesus accomplished belongs to us 100 percent. However, it is now our job to bring those things into manifestation in every area of our lives, and it has to be done by force (see Matt. 11:12).

Sometimes we are so religiously blinded that we cannot see the effects of Adam and Eve's sin in our lives.

Let us take the simple example of childbirth. How many women who are filled with the Holy Spirit and pursue holiness do you know who have delivered a child without pain? Most likely there are very few among us, because we consider it "normal" for women to have pain when giving birth. In our religious zeal, we forget that this pain is a curse that can be traced back all the way to Adam and Eve (see Gen. 3:16). Jesus has carried every curse on the cross for us, so having pain when delivering children should no longer be the status quo for us as believers. This curse came in the earth because Adam and Eve had removed themselves from the covenant with God. Through their agreement, they entered a covenant with the snake. And the curse that came forth as a result of it still exists in our lives today.

I believe that this curse was also destroyed and overcome, because Jesus did not miss a single curse on the cross. We must acquire this freedom through bloodline prayer. This is why it is one of our biggest concerns to see the full manifestation of the victory of Jesus Christ in the life of Christians.

Can you imagine what an amazing testimony it would be if Christian women came to hospitals and delivered their children without any pain! Simply because Jesus broke that curse and we testify about the manifestation of the cross. Wow!

Our God has broken every curse and put everything under His feet. It is time that we see the full manifestation of this victory in the lives of His people.

SPIRITUAL AND NATURAL

"You have put all things in subjection under his feet." For in that He put all in subjection under him, He left nothing that is not put under him. But now we do not yet see all things put under him (Hebrews 2:8).

This is an amazing Scripture. Yet it includes a paradox. On one hand, it speaks about Jesus Christ, who has subjected everything under His feet and there is nothing that has not been put under His feet. On the other hand, the same writer says directly afterward that we do not yet see that everything has been made subject to Him.

So what is true then? Are all things subjected unto Him or are they not?

At this specific point we discover a precious revelation. In the supernatural spiritual realm Jesus has already completed everything 2,000 years ago; every principality and power has been subjected to Him. Nothing was left out. Jesus is King of kings and Lord of lords. This is a fact that cannot be changed.

However, if we look at the world we do not see a reflection of the Kingdom of God in hundreds and thousands of areas in our society and world. You could even say it appears to be quite the opposite—things seem to be fully in the hands of the enemy.

Why is this so, even though Jesus has completed everything and nothing needs to be done by Him anymore? This is where we should step in.

The earth is the Lord's, and all its fullness, the world and those who dwell therein (Psalms 24:1).

Here we see the earth is clearly God's property. Still, we see in the following Scripture that He has given it into our administration.

Then God blessed them, and God said to them, "Be fruitful and multiply; fill the earth and subdue it; have dominion over the fish of the sea, over the birds of the air, and over every living thing that moves on the earth" (Genesis 1:28).

God has turned the earth over into our hands and responsibility. Therefore, it is no longer God's responsibility to bring heaven to earth, but it is ours. God has already completed everything. His part of the task has been fulfilled.

Yes, it is true that everything is already subject to Jesus—all powers, principalities, governments, and every area in society. This is true from a spiritual point of view. However, now it is necessary that we bring those things into manifestation here on the earth. We must make this victory visible here on earth.

And the way we make it happen begins with prayer. Prayer is not a method we use to convince God about a matter. Neither do we pray hoping that if we pray long enough we can manipulate God to give us what we want. Neither does prayer mean begging God and hoping that He will finally have mercy on us and hear our prayer.

No. Prayer means that we position ourselves in a way that allows God to fulfill His plans. We thus enable God to fulfill His plans, the things that Jesus paid the price for 2,000 years ago. We become part of His salvation plan by aligning our lives in prayer with the principles of God.

CHAPTER 2

COVENANT WITH GOD

Do we simply believe in God or do we live in a covenant relationship with Him?

There is a vast difference between believing in God and being in a covenant with God. Believing in God does not necessarily mean that we are also in a covenant with God. You could also say that true faith is always faith that originates in a covenant with God, but you can believe in God without being in a covenant with Him.

You believe that there is one God. You do well. Even the demons believe—and tremble! (James 2:19)

We see that even demons believe in God and yet they are not in a covenant with Him. James makes a clear point that believing is not the same as being in a covenant. In verse 24, he even goes a step further and states that man is not justified by faith alone but by his works as well.

Does that mean that works are sufficient to be justified? Absolutely not. James is just telling us—true faith always goes hand in hand with works. It does not remain fruitless.

Do you see that faith was working together with his works, and by works faith was made perfect? (James 2:22)

The Greek word for faith is *pistos* and means that we put our full trust into something or someone and build our life on it. If you truly believe in something, your whole life is in alignment with it.

In the history of humanity, we have plenty of good and bad examples of people putting their entire trust into something and bringing their lives into alignment with it. Looking back at the last century provides enough examples to see what it means to really believe in something.

Martin Luther King, Jr., for instance, became a crucial instrument in fighting segregation in the United States.

Dietrich Bonhoeffer rejected the regime in Nazi Germany because of his faith in the Bible, which cost him his life.

We have multiple examples of people who risked their lives, some even losing it, because they hid Jews. They believed, and because of their faith they were activated and resisted injustice.

We enjoy the benefits of those people who gave room to the Holy Spirit while facing tremendous persecution. One example is the outpouring of the Holy Spirit in Los Angeles, where in 1906 the Azusa Street revival took place, and there are many others more.

But there are also negative examples. Some people brought tremendous suffering to humanity because of their convictions, some even leading to the destruction of entire societies. Hitler murdered 6 million Jews and is mainly responsible for the 50 million deaths during World War II. Mao Zedong, China's leading politician, is responsible for the murder of up to 70 million people. Stalin during the Russian empire; the Khmer Rouge regime in Cambodia; the genocides of the Hutu against the Tutsi in Rwanda. There is also the genocide of the Armenians by the government of the Ottoman Empire, just to name a few examples from the last century.

All these examples show us clearly—if you really believe in something, you bring your life into alignment with it. It reveals whether you simply believe in something or whether you are someone who is in a covenant with it. If you are in a covenant relationship with God, you bring your entire life into alignment with Him. And if you pay the price for your faith you bring forth the fruit of your faith. You are convinced about Him and His leadership and you trust His entire being—the goodness, power, and might of God Almighty.

NOT JUST ELOHIM—YHWH

If you want to be successful in the redemption of your bloodline, the main requirement is to be in a covenant with God or decide to be in a covenant with Him.

To be in a covenant with God means that we have fellowship with God the Father, the Son, and the Holy Spirit. He barges into our lives and tells us where we should go. He gives orders and directions. He comforts us when we are hurt and He encourages us when we are demotivated. He strengthens us when we are weak and He helps us when we do not know how to go on. He is our king, our friend, our hero, our lawyer, our comforter, our Lord, and much more.

Being in a covenant with God means truly experiencing God.

Most of us know the following story from Genesis and we can probably also retell it ourselves. Yet if we have a closer look at those Scriptures, we will discover an interesting detail about the Hebrew name by which God is called.

> *Then the Lord God took the man and put him in the garden of Eden to tend and keep it. And the Lord God commanded the man, saying, "Of every tree of the garden you may freely eat; but of the tree of the knowledge of good and evil you shall not eat, for in the day that you eat of it you shall surely die"* (Genesis 2:15-17).

It says here that the Lord God put man in the Garden of Eden. He is not simply called God, but He is explicitly called the Lord God.

What is so amazing about this? "God" is a translation of the Hebrew word *elohim*. The word "Lord" is used to translate the Hebrew word *YHWH*, which stands for Yahweh. This word does not only mean God; it actually is the personal name of God. It is the name that God would use to show that there is an established covenant between Him and a particular person or nation.

For example, if we read that the *Lord God* spoke to Moses, it implies that there is a covenant relationship between God and Moses.

We will later examine the story of Balaam. It is interesting to note that the Bible never speaks about the Lord God with regard to Balaam. Every time it simply says that God spoke to Balaam. It shows us that Balaam did not enter a covenant with God. He believed in God and he heard God's voice clearly, but he did not bring his life into alignment with Him. Actually, his personal gain was more important to him.

Entering a covenant implies that we separate ourselves from everything that could break or breach that covenant. You even go a step further and live a life that testifies that we are in a covenant.

Consecrate yourselves therefore, and be holy, for I am the Lord your God (Leviticus 20:7).

Marriage is a great example. It is a covenant for life. If you enter this covenant, you automatically align your life and daily routine with it. If you want to successfully live in the marriage covenant, you must start living more selflessly than before. You must actively engage in that marriage to make it comfortable, enjoyable, and desirable. You put a ring on your finger to demonstrate that you are in a covenant relationship. This is how you protect yourself from other possible offers or relationships. You demonstrate and prove your faithfulness toward your partner. The enemy—the accuser, the devil, satan—and all the demons try to get us out of the covenant with God. They sprinkle doubt, lies, bitterness, and temptations. They want us to disconnect from our covenant with God. It is their goal to bring us to a place where we can be bound by the powers of darkness. This is exactly what the snake managed to do with Adam and Eve.

After God created everything, the Word of God calls him the *Lord God*, not just God. The fact that the author of Genesis uses God's personal name, which is only used when He is referred to as a covenant partner, emphasizes that God has entered a covenant with the entire creation.

God's covenants are so extensive and multifaceted that God revealed them to humanity step by step.

Abraham was in a covenant with God. God revealed Himself to him in Genesis 22 as Yahweh-Jireh, God our provider. We see that God had been faithful to this covenant, which included provision in Abraham's life.

He revealed himself to the Israelites in Exodus 15:26 as Yahweh-Rapha, God our healer. And we see that God was faithful to His covenant promises.

Your garments did not wear out on you, nor did your foot swell these forty years (Deuteronomy 8:4).

He also brought them out with silver and gold, and there was none feeble among His tribes (Psalms 105:37).

God's covenant with Israel secured their provision supernaturally during their time in the desert. In all those 40 years, their clothes did not wear out and they had no sicknesses nor diseases as long as they remained in that covenant.

The covenant with God was so strong that the Israelites had no sick or feeble person in their midst when they left Egypt, in spite of their suffering from beatings, terror, and the capriciousness of Pharaoh. This shows us that if we enter a covenant with God, He is faithful and just and He will not disappoint us.

We see more covenants in Exodus 17:15 where God revealed Himself as Yahweh-Nissi, the Lord my banner. In Exodus 20, we get to know Him as Yahweh Ha-Kodesh, the Lord who sanctifies us. In Judges 6:24, He is called Yahweh-Shalom, the Lord our peace. In Psalms 23:1, God reveals Himself as Yahweh-Rapha, the Lord our shepherd. In Ezekiel 48:35, He is Yahweh-Shammah, the Lord who is here.

All those Scriptures reveal the blessings that are available for us when we enter a covenant with God. Look at all these blessings that are included in the covenant with God. No wonder the devil makes such an effort to push us out of the covenant with God.

MAN AND THE SNAKE

Yet, this was exactly the way the snake was successful with Eve.

Now the serpent was more cunning than any beast of the field which the Lord God had made. And he said to the woman, "Has God indeed said, 'You shall not eat of every tree of the garden'?" And the woman said to the serpent, "We may eat the fruit of the trees of the garden; but of the fruit of the tree which is in the midst of the garden, God has said, 'You shall not eat it, nor shall you touch it, lest you die.'"

Then the serpent said to the woman, "You will not surely die. For God knows that in the day you eat of it your eyes will be opened, and you will be like God, knowing good and evil" (Genesis 3:1-5).

The snake had thought up a deceitful plan—it tried to seduce Eve out of the area of her covenant with God. This has been the devil's plan from the beginning; nothing has changed since.

When the snake talked about God, it didn't call Him the *Lord God* but simply *God*. By avoiding His covenant name *Yahweh*, it tried to lure Eve out of the realm of her covenant with God. This is how the enemy played down the necessity of the covenant of God as well as its promises, including His goodness and protection. If you want to seduce people you don't necessarily have to make up lies; often it is enough if you don't provide the full truth. That was the strategy of the serpent. Using the word *God* sounded pretty good and right; however, it undermined the important part of the covenant with Him.

The snake tries to do the exact same thing today. It attaches itself to man's ego and stubbornness and feeds it. The snake has no problem when people simply believe in God. It would have been hard to convince Eve that there is no God, because she spent time with Him daily. Subsequently, it is not a problem for the enemy if people believe in God. The problem arises when people decide to enter a covenant relationship with God and align their lives with Him. It shakes up the kingdom of darkness. It starts a process that causes the kingdoms of this world to be transformed into the Kingdoms of our God and of His Christ.

The kingdoms of this world have become the kingdoms of our Lord and of His Christ, and He shall reign forever and ever! (Revelation 11:15)

Unfortunately, Eve's reaction was not a confession toward *the Lord God*. She took the bait of the enemy. Even though she tried to put the statement in the right light, in her conversation with the snake she did not refer to the *Lord God* but simply to God. She did not stand on the covenant, but she stepped outside of the realm of this covenant. She could have pointed the snake back into its proper boundaries and confessed her covenant relationship with the *Lord God*. Through its craftiness the snake had managed to lower the value of the covenant with God in Eve's eyes. And that was exactly how Eve was shifted out of the sphere of the covenant with God. She distanced herself from God and entered a different sphere in which the enemy could seduce her. She removed herself from God's sphere and shifted into a sphere where she could be seduced. This is how she lost the covenant blessings of God, His abundance, and His boundlessness. Please note that it was not God who limited the abundance of His covenant.

And they heard the sound of the Lord God walking in the garden in the cool of the day, and Adam and his wife hid themselves from the presence of the Lord God among the trees of the garden.

Then the Lord God called to Adam and said to him, "Where are you?" (Genesis 3:8-9)

Right after the Fall the Bible still speaks about the *Lord God*. God is continually faithful to His covenant and nothing has changed about it. It is His desire to fulfill it. Man had distanced himself from it. It is up to man whether he wants to get the full measure of the blessings of God and live in them. God's will and passion have not changed after the Fall. To confirm this, He continues to call himself *the Lord God*.

BALAAM HEARD GOD, BUT HAD NO COVENANT WITH HIM

Earlier in this book, I wrote about Balaam and that he was not in a covenant with God. We can read about him in Numbers 22. The story is about Balak, king of Moab, who was afraid of the Israelites. He was in fear because he had heard how Israel had, step by step, taken more and more land. To stop this conquest of land he called for Balaam, who back then had been a famous fortuneteller. Balak's goal was to make Balaam curse the people of God. And this is where the interesting part of the story begins.

First of all, note that Balaam heard the voice of God. The Word of God clearly says so.

Second, note that he echoed the word he heard correctly. But the third thing to note is that he tried to curse Israel several times, because Balak was able to talk him into doing so. Did he figure God would waver and change His mind? Obviously, his personal gain played a significant role in this event.

Fourth, Balaam found a way to seduce Israel out of their protection by God. He suggested to the Moabites that they send their daughters into the camp of the Israelites. When they did so, they seduced the Israelites to fornication and to idolatry. And that's how the people of God brought a curse on themselves.

We see that Balaam repeated the Word of God accurately, yet he tried to bypass it. His life was concentrated on compromise for his personal gain.

The fifth point shows us clearly that even though Balaam heard God he was not in a covenant with Him. All through this story we read that God always speaks as "Elohim" and never as "Yahweh" with Balaam. If someone was in covenant relationship with God, He would at least once have referred to Himself as *Lord God*, Yahweh, who spoke with this person.

In Numbers 8:1, the *Lord God* speaks with Moses. In Joshua 1:1, the *Lord God* speaks with Joshua. In Genesis 18:13, the *Lord God* speaks with Abraham. In Judges 7:2, the *Lord God* speaks with Gideon. In First Samuel 3:11, the *Lord God* speaks to Samuel, etc. Yet we never see that the *Lord God* spoke with Balaam. Scripture simply mentions that "God" spoke with Balaam, which clarifies that there was no covenant between Balaam and God.

It is interesting to see that Balaam appears to have believed about himself that he has a covenant with God. Because when he prophesies he speaks about the *Lord God* as the one who had spoken to him. So the problem is that Balaam thought that he was in a covenant with God even though he actually wasn't.

This is a significant story. It illustrates how important it is that we have a relationship with God and that we allow the Holy Spirit to get to our hearts. The Holy Spirit was given to us so we can be cleansed, sanctified, and renewed. It can be very tricky if we walk in the gifts of the Holy Spirit, if we speak prophetically and demonstrate signs and wonders, but we do not cultivate a passionate personal relationship with God. We may think about ourselves that everything is fine, because God uses us by working through His gifts. However, the Bible says that those gifts and callings are irrevocable, no matter what the lifestyle of a person may be like. Working signs and wonders therefore is not necessarily a confirmation for a healthy walk with God. We can be blinded by those gifts and also blind others. And that was the condition Balaam found himself in.

Where do I want to go with this? God's goal and heart is that we would not only know and hear Him, but that we would also follow Him. God is not Santa, whom we approach when we want something. God is the Lord and we are His children. He wants to have a relationship with us. He wants to teach us how to overcome, pursue Him, love, and keep His ways and commands as we abandon ourselves completely to Him. Abandon ourselves to Him even if we have personal requests that appear to be more important to us. He desires that we give ourselves to Him, including our personal gain and our personal desires. If we lose our life, we will win it. This is the promise God has given us.

This is the foundation to have successful bloodline prayer. And it is also the foundation to be successful in the courts of heaven. (I will examine the terminology of *courts of heaven* in Chapter 5.)

Those prayers are not a method to help us fulfill our personal and selfish desires. The foundation of everything is the personal relationship with God, our love and dedication to Him, and a personal covenant with the Lord God. That's how we are being led to be and live out what God has written in the book of our life before the foundation of the world.

I would now ask you to take some personal time with the Lord. Enter the presence of God and ask Him to expand His covenant with you in all areas of your life. Ask Him to become the Lord over each area of your life. Detach yourself from all selfish desires and ideas that you wanted to use God for. Come to that place where you tell God that if the death of Jesus is the only thing He would ever give you, it is still more than anything we have ever deserved.

God does not owe us anything. But we know that He has given His only Son to us, and everything else in addition to that. If we give up our own desires and requests for the sake of the Kingdom we know that He will add all other things to us. If God asks something from us, He doesn't do it to take it away from us. He does it because He wants to bless us abundantly more than what we can ask or imagine.

We see that nothing has changed about God's covenant; it simply requests us to engage and become active by aligning our life and releasing the covenant of God over it.

When praying our bloodline, we implement this. We bring every area of our lives into alignment with the covenants of God. This also includes that we align the past of our forefathers all the way back to Adam with the covenants of God because they can still influence our lives today.

It is God's passion that His children live in the full manifestation of His covenant. If this isn't experienced, the problem many times is in the bloodline. We see people who are God-fearing, spirit-filled, and they even love God above everything, and yet many times they do not live in the fullness of the promises of God. Some not only do not live in them, but they also die without experiencing all the promises that belong to them.

It is time to become a testimony for Jesus that cannot be overlooked in this world. Because God says:

My covenant I will not break, nor alter the word that has gone out of My lips (Psalms 89:34).

CHAPTER 3

DISSOLVING COVENANTS

You shall make no covenant with them, nor with their gods. They shall not dwell in your land, lest they make you sin against Me. For if you serve their gods, it will surely be a snare to you (Exodus 23:32-33).

Our own guilt and iniquity have consequences in our lives. The same applies for the sin and iniquity of our forefathers. Those are things that we need to repent for because they can also restrict the lives of our children and children's children.

You shall not bow down to them nor serve them. For I, the Lord your God, am a jealous God, visiting the iniquity of the fathers upon the children to the third and fourth generations of those who hate Me, but showing mercy to thousands, to those who love Me and keep My commandments (Exodus 20:5-6).

Some sins create deep covenants that do not glorify God. In most cases, those are covenants with gods that release curses over the entire bloodline. Those things are much deeper and more tenacious than the iniquity reaching back to the third and fourth generation.

During my travels to Asia, I can observe this regularly. For centuries, other gods have been worshiped by which people and regions have been brought into captivity. Those gods do not only keep people in captivity, they also try to choke down truth and to destroy. Many decades ago covenants were made with these gods. They are still in effect today, which is why they need to be dissolved in the spirit. Dissolving these covenants will pave the way to allow love and freedom to abound there.

In the Bible, we read about plenty of covenants. We see covenants that God has with man. And we also see plenty of covenants that man made with man or a people of another nation.

The great biblical covenants are the covenant of Adam, the covenant of Noah, the covenant of Abraham, the covenant of Moses, the covenant of David, and the New Covenant that is mainly known as the New Testament. Some would even consider the covenant with the land of Canaan as one of the covenants. It is not the theme of this book to present those covenants; however, providing this list clarifies that the relationship of God to man was established on those covenants.

It is also important for our understanding that we discern between conditional and unconditional covenants. The covenant of Adam is an unconditional covenant. It means that God has made an eternal covenant with humanity—He will never stop taking care of man and searching for him. This covenant is unconditional.

The covenant of Moses, on the other hand, is activated by sticking to its conditions. It means that resolute action is required to activate it.

Behold, I set before you today a blessing and a curse: the blessing, if you obey the commandments of the Lord your God which I command you today; and the curse, if you do not obey the commandments of the Lord your God, but turn aside from the way which I command you today, to go after other gods which you have not known (Deuteronomy 11:26-28).

Now it shall come to pass, if you diligently obey the voice of the Lord your God, to observe carefully all His commandments which I command you today, that the Lord your God will set you high above all nations of the earth. And all these blessings shall come upon you and overtake you, because you obey the voice of the Lord your God (Deuteronomy 28:1-2).

There are four ways covenants are established. The Bible speaks about blood covenants, seed covenants, salt covenants, and word or meal covenants. Blood covenants have the greatest connections.

Later in this chapter, I will go into these four categories of covenants in more detail. We want to understand why it is so important that we should break off from those covenants—even covenants our ancestors may have made generations ago.

BERIYTH

The Hebrew word for covenant is *beriyth*. For centuries, there has been extensive consideration about the word stem or the root of this word *beriyth*. Some are of the opinion that *beriyth* is derived from the word *barah*. *Barah* means *to eat*. This is interesting as every covenant ceremony is accompanied by feasting with a meal.

Baru is another word stem that could be the root word for *covenant*. *Baru* means to *choose, determine, to obligate*.

The most likely explanation for the word appears to be *biritu*. Biritu means band or shackle.

I will make you pass under the rod, and I will bring you into the bond of the covenant (Ezekiel 20:37)

I won't be able to come up with a word definition that is 100 percent certain here. However, what matters to us is that every reflection about the word stem has its reason to exist. Every possibility presented describes the part of a ceremony of a covenant. Feasting, destiny, obligation, band, or shackle—all of these are characteristics for a covenant.

A covenant is not simply a loose agreement of two or more parties. It is a vow, with a destiny and an obligation that involves, binds, and shackles you as well as your descendants. It is active as long as there are any descendants from you. We are talking about destinies and purposes that undeniably influence your everyday life as well as your decisions.

DAVID AND JONATHAN

David had made a covenant with Jonathan.

Then Jonathan and David made a covenant, because he loved him as his own soul (1 Samuel 18:3).

In First Samuel 20:16, we read that even though this covenant was between David and Jonathan personally, it had an effect on both of their households. All descendants of David and Jonathan had entered a covenant relationship as well. It was a binding and undeniable covenant.

Now David said, "Is there still anyone who is left of the house of Saul, that I may show him kindness for Jonathan's sake?" (2 Samuel 9:1)

This covenant was very important to David and brought obligations as well, even during his reign as a king. A few years after having been crowned he wanted to make sure that he would keep this covenant. He personally was not aware of any descendants of Jonathan that were still alive. So he did a research about it to make sure there really weren't any.

JONATHANS' SON MEPHIBOSHETH

David was surprised to find out that Jonathan's son Mephibosheth was still alive. Due to an accident, Mephibosheth was lame in both legs. It occurred when his nanny fled when she heard about Saul and Jonathan's death. Those are strange circumstances, because if she had known that there was a covenant between David and Jonathan she may never have fled and this accident would not have happened. What a tragic incident because his nanny was not aware of the existing covenant.

The Bible says that the people of God perish because of their lack of knowledge (see Hos. 4:6). The life of Mephibosheth is such a good example and still very typical. Most Christians do not know that they have a covenant with Him and consequently do not live in the fullness of those blessings.

Mephibosheth lived in Lo Debar after his escape. *Lo Debar* means "pastureless" and it describes the area and the circumstances in which he lived. He grew up in poverty even though there was a covenant that secured wealth for him. Jonathan's son lived in a battle for daily provision even though this covenant included provision and even servants for him. He lived with a low reputation even though the covenant of his father promised tremendous reputation for him.

Even today, Christians many times live a life that is not in agreement with the covenant that Jesus has made. On the one hand, it is because they do not understand the contents of the covenant due to the blood, the cross, and the resurrection of Jesus Christ, and they will never be told about it. On the other hand, they do not understand how to dissolve bad covenants from their forefathers. Many do not know that those covenants are still active and affect their life.

We may think that because we are Christians, bad covenants cannot influence us. Or that God does not regard them any longer. On the one hand, it is true that Jesus has completely set us free from every bad covenant that our ancestors may have made. But on the other hand, there are many areas in our lives where we have to take action and need to step out. We have to actively apply what Jesus released for us.

The Bible says in First Peter 2:24 that we have been healed by the stripes of Jesus. This means that Jesus has already healed every person from their sickness and disease. Yet we see so many Christians suffering and dying of diseases that have tortured them for years. Why? The reason for this can be that the healing Jesus released for everybody often has to be taken by faith and by force. This is the way it is with many covenants.

GOD RECOGNIZES AND RESPECTS COVENANTS

The Gibeonites were a people in Canaan, the land that God had promised that the Israelites would take step by step. But God said that the Israelites should not make a covenant with any of the people of that land.

When the Gibeonites found out how powerfully the Israelites advanced in taking the land and the area, they made a plan to outwit them. They wanted to enter into a covenant with them. That's why they sent their representatives who approached them.

And it happened at the end of three days, after they had made a covenant with them, that they heard that they were their neighbors who dwelt near them (Joshua 9:16).

At their arrival they lied to the Israelites about their identity, origin, and ethnicity. The people of God believed that lie and made a covenant with them. It was because of this covenant that the Israelites could not conquer the land of the Gibeonites. And when the Israelites realized their mistake it was too late, because the covenants were already in place. They had to respect this covenant, even though it had been wrong.

Then all the rulers said to all the congregation, "We have sworn to them by the Lord God of Israel; now therefore, we may not touch them" (Joshua 9:19).

What had happened was not the will of God. In verse 14, we are also shown that the Israelites had not asked God about it. They came to this conclusion out of their own persuasion.

The amazing thing is how God saw this covenant. This covenant was not in agreement with the will of God, so you might think that God would not recognize it. Yet the opposite is the case.

> *Now there was a famine in the days of David for three years, year after year; and David inquired of the Lord. And the Lord answered, "It is because of Saul and his bloodthirsty house, because he killed the Gibeonites"* (2 Samuel 21:1).

Because Israel had made a covenant with the Gibeonites, this covenant was legal, even though it had not been the will of God to establish it in the first place. But God's righteousness and His justice do not allow anything else but for established covenants to be honored.

We can see that God judges the Israelites about 350 years later because of this covenant, even though this covenant was outside of His will. When Saul disregarded that covenant and killed the Gibeonites, God judged the Israelites on the basis of this covenant. Consequently, a famine came to Israel.

COVENANTS ARE VALID UNTIL DEATH

What is the solution for wrong covenants and how can we get released from them? The only possibility we have left is death. There is no other way out.

Does that mean that we will stay in these covenants until we die? Yes and no!

Yes, because there is no other way out, and no because we have died with Christ through our salvation and baptism. There was a death that can take us out of our covenants.

All covenants were cancelled and dissolved through our salvation, our decision for Christ, and our baptism. As mentioned already, this is not a fact that can be easily dissolved. However, we have to activate this status for our natural circumstances, which happens when we use repentance to annul their power.

Many covenants were erased immediately through our salvation and baptism. But we must admit that, in spite of our salvation and baptism, the consequences and effects are still bothering us. In those cases, we must dissolve the precise covenant, which happens through repentance in bloodline prayer.

Mephibosheth had to activate his rights personally even though the privileges existed before he did so. He had a covenant working in his life, but he did not live within its blessings. The problem was not in the covenant; the problem was the lack of activation of this covenant.

On September 22, 1862, the American government declared the abolition of slavery under Abraham Lincoln. When General Gordon Granger read this declaration and the Declaration of Emancipation in Galveston, Texas, on June 19, 1865, it was two and a half years since the original release thereof. However, the slaves in Texas had continued to live under the yoke of slavery during those two-and-a-half years and continuously worked for their masters because the slave owners consciously withheld the information about this release from them. Even though the slaves legally were no longer slaves, they could not enjoy their freedom because they did not know what had been ascribed to them.

What a great example to explain what is going on in the spirit world. Today thousands of Christians live imprisoned, because they do not really realize what Jesus has done for them on the cross and they do not know how to apply the completed work of Jesus in their lives. That is also how demons try their best to hide this truth from Christians.

It is time to activate the full extent of the power of the blood of Jesus, the cross, and the covenants.

BLOOD COVENANTS

Blood covenants have the greatest impact of all covenants. The Bible tells us that there is life in the blood (see Lev. 17:11). Therefore, those covenants are based on the most precious foundation of all, which is life.

Certainly, the covenant that we have in Jesus Christ is the most glorious one that ever existed. It required the most precious price that has ever been paid—the life of the Son of God. Jesus paid with His life so we can have health, glory, freedom, truth, and life for free. Getting it for free should not be mixed up with the fact that there was a price that had to be paid for it. It cost our Messiah losing His life through crucifixion. This covenant, established by blood at the cross, is so brilliant and perfect that all powers and principalities must bow before Him.

When we look at what Abel did we see that people knew from the very beginning that blood covenants have the greatest impact of all covenants. Abel offered the first fruit of his herds to the Lord. God was so pleased and looked at his offering. When Abel was killed by his brother Cain, his blood still spoke and God confirmed it. This was possible because by faith Abel had entered a covenant with God.

Abel had decided to become a shepherd because establishing a covenant with God was so important to him. At that time, there was no reason to be a shepherd. At that time only Adam, Eve, Cain, and Abel lived on the earth. They did not need a room full of clothes, so clothing was not a reason for being a shepherd. People started to eat meat only after the flood (see Gen. 9:39), so provision for food could not have been a reason for shepherding either. The only reason that was left was to approach God by bringing an offering and to keep the covenant with Him. This is the reason Abel decided to become a shepherd.

Noah was another righteous man of God who had entered a blood covenant with God. The Word of God says that Noah was supposed to take two of each kind of animal into the ark—a male and a female. This fact is common knowledge even among children. However, few people have noticed that in Genesis 7:2 God commands Noah to take seven of every clean animal. Why should he take seven or seven pairs (this is up for debate) of each clean animal and just one pair of every unclean one? The answer is connected to the covenant that Noah made with God after the waters had returned.

Then Noah built an altar to the Lord, and took of every clean animal and of every clean bird, and offered burnt offerings on the altar. And the Lord smelled a soothing aroma. Then the Lord said in His heart, "I will never again curse the ground for man's sake, although the imagination of man's heart is evil from his youth; nor will I again destroy every living thing as I have done" (Genesis 8:20-21).

Noah opened the ark and allowed all the animals to exit. But immediately he built an altar to the Lord. On this altar, he brought burnt offerings of the clean animals he had taken into the ark. He used them to establish a blood covenant with God—a covenant that is established for all generations to come.

Then God spoke to Noah and to his sons with him, saying: "And as for Me, behold, I establish My covenant with you and with your descendants after you, and with every living creature that is with you: the birds, the cattle, and every beast of the earth with you, of all that go out of the ark, every beast of the earth. Thus I establish My covenant with you: Never again shall all flesh be cut off by the waters of the flood; never again shall there be a flood to destroy the earth" (Genesis 9:8-11).

This covenant was made in Genesis 8:21 when Noah offered clean animals and this offering ascended as a sweet fragrance to the Lord. To this day, the rainbow is a reminder that we have this covenant and it is an eternal one.

We see Abraham, Moses, David, and many others who entered a blood covenant with God that still impacts us today. There are also covenants that we need to resign from because they have negative effects on our lives. They are not pleasant for us as human beings; neither are they pleasant to God.

Then he took his eldest son who would have reigned in his place, and offered him as a burnt offering upon the wall; and there was great indignation against Israel. So they departed from him and returned to their own land (2 Kings 3:27).

To me this is one of the most brutal incidents that is described in the Bible. Being the father of a son, it is hard for me to imagine what could cause a father to do such a cruel thing. But this story explains a lot about blood covenants to us.

After Ahab, the king of Israel, died, the king of Moab broke his covenant with him. Then King Jehoram, who was Ahab's descendant, went to King Jehoshaphat, king of Judah, to win this battle. King Jehoshaphat agreed and they both went against Moab with their armies. At a point of discouragement Jehoshaphat suggested they ask a prophet about the outcome of the battle. When they asked the prophet Elisha, he spoke the word of the Lord to them and confirmed their victory (see 2 Kings 3:19). The accuracy of the prophecy was confirmed by a miracle the following morning.

Now it happened in the morning, when the grain offering was offered, that suddenly water came by way of Edom, and the land was filled with water (2 Kings 3:20).

Just as the prophet had predicted, the Israelites became witnesses of what the prophet had seen, so they moved back into battle full of faith. They fought and overcame just as Elisha had foretold it, in every fight. But then what I mentioned above happened—the king of Moab saw that the battle was too heavy and that he was about to lose. So he took his firstborn son and sacrificed him as a burnt offering on the wall. When the Israelites saw this, they got very angry. They were so shaken up by this event that they pulled back from the fight and turned away.

Isn't it astonishing that they walked from victory to victory just like the prophet had predicted it? But when they saw the king of Moab offering his own son, it influenced their hearts, their motivation, and their focus. In other words, the blood offering or the blood covenant of the Moabite king fulfilled its purpose.

The Israelites had witnessed and committed similar crimes under King Ahab, so the reason they pulled back was not simply the cruelty of the king sacrificing his own son. It was the power of the blood offering.

Israel had gone to war against Moab and even had the confirmation and word of God about it. They had a prophecy that they would be successful. But the power of the offering of the Moabite king influenced the hearts of the Israelites in such a way that it hindered them from completing their mission. Here we see the power of blood covenants—even covenants that are not pleasing to the Lord can have legal influence.

Allow me to explain briefly why the offering of the king of Moab had the power to turn around the hearts of the Israelites. In verse 20 of this chapter, we see how the Israelites had brought an offering that morning before leaving for battle. This was custom according to the law of Moses. It was not unusual. However, if you read the law of the ritual for morning offerings, you will notice something.

According to Numbers 28 and Exodus 29:39-42, the law requires they bring a food offering and add a lamb offering as well every morning and every evening. Offering a lamb and a burnt offering was a daily confirmation of the covenant with God. However, this morning the Israelites had only brought a food offering and dropped the burnt offering. They had neglected and overlooked the most powerful form of a covenant—the blood covenant. The Moabite king had brought a higher form of offering and an offering with greater weight. This helped the king to get victory even though Israel was supposed to win.

My friend Adeyemi Adefarasin from Nigeria once preached a message entitled "The heavens belong to the highest bidder." Using this story, he explains that we should not think that no effort is needed from our side. If we want to spread the Kingdom of God on the earth, getting personally engaged is a requirement. Satan and his armies as well as his followers among men bring great sacrifices in order to exclude the glory of the Lord from mankind—in particular the children of God.

We desire to see God's glory, dominion, government, and kingdom increase and expand on the earth. But this also means that the sons of God must arise and fulfill the assignment of Jesus. The Bible says in Revelation that we have overcome the accuser through the blood of the Lamb and the word of our testimony, but also by not loving our lives unto death. In addition to the existing sacrifice of Jesus there is another sacrifice listed here that we need to bring. It is an offering that reflects our everyday life and at which we also lay down our lives. In Hebrews 11 and 12, we see the cloud of witnesses or heroes of faith who surround us. Those are people who already lived a selfless life out of love and faith for God and who brought sacrifices in their own lives.

When praying bloodlines one of the things we are doing is dissolving blood covenants. Blood covenants may have been established by ourselves, but they may also have been established by our ancestors. Covenants still have negative effects on us to this day and keep us bound up in various areas of our lives.

Establishing those covenants may have happened through murder or raising blood altars for other gods, but also through killing crusades in a god's name; they also include abortions and much more. I will elaborate on this in the second part of this book.

SEED COVENANTS

The next thing I would like to do is to mention seed covenants. Those are covenants that are established by sexual relationships, at which seed is being released. Seed covenants can be considered a part of the blood covenant and according to my studies seed covenants have the second greatest effect.

If we look at the Word of God and stories about sexual acts that were done outside the principles and order of God, we can see terrible effects. Effects that can last for centuries and even to this day.

One of illegitimate birth shall not enter the assembly of the Lord; even to the tenth generation none of his descendants shall enter the assembly of the Lord (Deuteronomy 23:2).

So, it says here that someone who was born out of wedlock cannot come into the assembly of the Lord all the way down to the tenth generation. At first glance this appears to be very strict and exaggerated. However, my emphasis is that we should get an understanding about the consequences a sexual relationship has if it is not done according to the law of God. The consequences were not only passed down to the third and fourth generation, but at least to the tenth generation. This is unmistakably a form of a curse. But it also reveals to us how important sexuality is in the sight of God.

When reading the Word of God we can find a number of stories about seed covenants and their consequences. They have great significance for us today. The connections of those events reveal and explain the value and holiness that God ascribes to sexuality.

Abraham begot his son Ishmael from his concubine Hagar, which was outside of the law and order of God. Two nations came forth from him, the Arabs and the Israelites. The effect of these seed covenants can be seen to this day in the conflict between Israel and the Arab world.

At Balaam's advice, the daughters of Moab were sent into the camp of the Israelites to seduce them into fornication and into bringing offerings to other gods. Balaam's cunning advice was the only possibility to pull the people of Israel out of their covenant with God. And as they entered into seed covenants they left the protection of the Most High. As a result they had to experience the consequences of this self-inflicted curse in all severity—24,000 Israelites died due to a plague.

Let us go one step further and talk about Moab. Who were those Moabites, who could commit fornication with the Israelites?

Moab was Lot's firstborn son. He was born after Lot had fled from Sodom and Gomorrah. Lot's wife had turned into a pillar of salt, and he kept going with his two daughters on his own. Being afraid that they might not get their own descendants, these daughters got their father drunk, took advantage of his state of drunkenness, and committed incest. Moab was born as a result of it.

We read in the Bible that the people of Moab were known for fornication and perverted idolatry. You could say they carried this sin in their bloodline. The effects of the sexual covenant between Lot and his daughters can be seen here, even 6,000 years later. It brought tremendous guilt and sorrow upon the people of Israel.

We also see the tragedies in David's family because of the many marriages he had. Naturally every marriage was a seed covenant. The result of these covenants was murder, rape, hate, and ungodliness. David's son Ammon raped his half-sister Tamar (see 2 Sam. 13:14). Ammon was later killed by the command his brother Absalom had given (see 2 Sam. 13:28). Absalom slept with all the wives of his father in the sight of all of Israel (see 2 Sam. 16:22). And David's son Solomon turned to idolatry (see 1 Kings 11:4).

The wisdom of God was in Solomon like in no other person on earth before him. But the uncountable seed covenants he made turned him away from God toward idolatry and ungodliness. This led to Israel's split in two kingdoms, the northern kingdom of Israel and the southern kingdom of Judah. And eventually it led to the complete destruction of Israel.

All these stories tell us that consequences and iniquity from seed covenants can have effects for centuries and millennia and they can only be erased by the redemption of Jesus Christ.

MERCY ABOVE LAW

Even regarding the seed covenants the mercy of God is revealed in Scripture. I want to take David's rulership as an example for how the grace and mercy of God are above the law.

According to the law written in Deuteronomy 23:3-4, King David should never have become king. On the foundation of this law he was disqualified, because we see in his family tree in Matthew 1:3 that David was in the ninth generation after Perez. Yet Perez was born out of a "one night stand" between Judah and his daughter-in-law Tamar. So according to the law, David was not qualified to become king. Only his grandchild, being the eleventh generation, would have had a legitimate right to become king.

We can add another level to this drama—Ruth, the great-grandmother of David, was a Moabite. The descendant of a Moabite could not become king either. This also have meant breaking the law, which made it impossible for David to become king.

To show even more how much he was disqualified, I want to add the fact that it is very likely that David himself was a child born out of wedlock. This may have been the reason why he was busy looking after the sheep and his dad did not consider him as one of the sons that Samuel might want to anoint as king.

It sounds like David confirms this line of thought when he says:

Behold, I was brought forth in iniquity, and in sin my mother conceived me (Psalms 51:5).

When we look at all these circumstances of David's life, he was the least qualified for the office of the king of Israel. No matter how you look at it, there were too many reasons why he should not have become king. Yet God looked at David's heart and saw his character, which reflected Him. And in His grace, mercy, and love He redeemed the bloodline of David to qualify him for the greatest office of authority in the world back then.

What a tremendous picture of God's love and greatness. This event encourages us even more to freely step before the throne of grace.

WORD AND MEAL COVENANTS

These covenants are a combination of giving one's word to someone and confirming it with a meal. This is also the way God entered a covenant with Israel and the elders.

Then Moses went up, also Aaron, Nadab, and Abihu, and seventy of the elders of Israel, and they saw the God of Israel. And there was under His feet as it were a paved work of sapphire stone, and it was like the very heavens in its clarity. But on the nobles of the children of Israel He did not lay His hand. So they saw God, and they ate and drank (Exodus 24:9-11).

For many years, Exodus 24:9-11 was one of my favorite Scriptures; I was fascinated by it. It amazes me that someone can experience God and still eat at the same time! I think I would have forgotten my food and just stared with mouth wide open and eyes glued on Him while taking in the experience.

The word and meal covenant included ceremonies like exchanging armors, coats, and sometimes even the firstborn. Unfortunately, it would go beyond the scope of this book to go into further detail about these things.

The covenant Jesus made with us is also connected to a meal—communion.

Then Jesus said to them, "Most assuredly, I say to you, unless you eat the flesh of the Son of Man and drink His blood, you have no life in you. Whoever eats My flesh and drinks My blood has eternal life, and I will raise him up at the last day" (John 6:53-54).

Communion is of great significance to our covenant with God. Jesus even calls it vital. Communion is not simply a symbol of the death of Jesus and the resurrection. No, it is a powerful proclamation and confirmation of our covenant with Jesus. We declare that we do not submit to any other covenant or God.

Therefore whoever eats this bread or drinks this cup of the Lord in an unworthy manner will be guilty of the body and blood of the Lord. But let a man examine himself, and so let him eat of the bread and drink of the cup. For he who eats and drinks in an unworthy manner eats and drinks judgment to himself, not discerning the Lord's body. For this reason many are weak and sick among you, and many sleep (1 Corinthians 11:27-30).

The covenant of Jesus in communion is not just a simple symbol, but it is a powerful deed. The Corinthians underestimated its holiness and had to suffer the consequences.

This covenant is not made to harm us but to bless us, to elevate and enable us. However, there are revelations about how we correctly behave and position ourselves in these covenants. Because some of the Corinthians received communion in an unworthy manner they released a curse rather than a blessing on themselves. Subsequently many became sick and some even died.

We recognize here that communion releases the judgment of God. It is interesting that people, even Christians, only associate something negative with the judgments of God. This should not be the case for Christians. At court there are always two parties when judgment is released—a winning party and a losing one. Being God's covenant partners we expect to receive a good verdict, and we should think about the judgment of God with positive emotions.

Whenever we position ourselves rightly and in a worthy manner at communion, it releases a confirmation as well as a proclamation of our covenant with Jesus. And it causes God to bring judgment. The verdict of this judgment is in our favor because God is a righteous judge.

The meal covenant with Jesus and His flesh and blood is powerful. However, this amazing gift is being neglected around the world among Christians. Or it is just received like a dead tradition—or simply forgotten. If we understand that communion makes principalities and powers shake in their boots, and if the authority of communion once again becomes a lively part of church, we will make a large step forward in spreading the Kingdom of God on earth faster and more effectively.

In First Corinthians 10:21, we read that we should not participate at the table of demons. We understand from this context that it speaks about food here that is being dedicated to other gods and sacrificed to them.

There are many controversies among Christians about whether it is legal to take food that has been dedicated to demons or not. Let us take for example the halal meat of our Muslim citizens. This meat has been prepared according to a specific pattern of slaughtering, and at the same time it has been dedicated to Allah and therefore becomes meat offered to idols.

Most people do not mind eating halal meat, possibly out of ignorance. Some say we are free to eat everything. Yet some people say that you should never eat meat offered to idols. Both sides have a few Scriptures to underscore what they consider to be truth from the Word of God.

This subject is a great subject for a substantiated biblical exegesis. The New Testament simply mentions it in six Scriptures. The sum of all Scriptures allows the following conclusion: Eating meat offered or dedicated to idols is acceptable. However, you must respect the conscience of your brothers and sisters. You may have to decline this meat for their sake. Yet it is forbidden to eat meat dedicated to idols during a ceremony that is taking place in honor of this idol. Participating in these ceremonies means entering into a covenant with this idol.

In First Corinthians 10:21, Scripture warns us that participating in such a ritual is not just equal to partaking at the table or cup of demons, but it literally means participating in them. We enter a meal covenant with demons by eating meat offered to idols during a ceremony.

Now you get an idea of how much cleansing is required from all the things we have carried in our bloodline since Adam. There are so many things that come from different eras and areas of idol worship.

Through their idolatry our ancestors established seed covenants as well as meal and word covenants that have effects on us to this day. I will expand on this in the next chapter.

WORD COVENANTS

Using the following event from the Bible, I want to point out the power of word covenants and their effects. They can have effects that last over centuries; actually, they exist until they are broken.

Then Joshua charged them at that time, saying, "Cursed be the man before the Lord who rises up and builds this city Jericho; he shall lay its foundation with his firstborn, and with his youngest he shall set up its gates" (Joshua 6:26).

Joshua's story shows us the power of word covenants or word curses very well. Joshua proclaimed this covenant over the land where Jericho had been established. He released a curse that was active for several centuries. When Jericho was rebuilt around 500 years later, its effect still caused suffering. According to First Kings 16:34, the word of Joshua was confirmed that he laid its foundation with his firstborn. This word covenant kept the land on which Jericho was built in bondage, so that the water in the city was bad and cost many unborn children their lives.

And the men of the city said to Elisha, Behold, inhabiting of this city is pleasant, as my lord sees, but the water is bad and the locality causes miscarriage and barrenness [in all animals].

He said, Bring me a new bowl and put salt [the symbol of God's purifying power] in it. And they brought it to him.

Then Elisha went to the spring of the waters and cast the salt in it and said, Thus says the Lord: I [not the salt] have healed these waters; there shall not be any more death, miscarriage or barrenness [and bereavement] because of it (2 Kings 2:19-21 AMPC).

The word covenant of Joshua became ineffective when Elisha broke the curse and established a salt covenant between God and Jericho.

SALT COVENANTS

Out of the four covenants we introduced we now get to the last covenant—the salt covenant. There are just around two or three, possibly four Scriptures that mention this covenant. We do not have a clear description of what and how a salt covenant is established. If we follow logic, however, we notice that salt is offered, poured out, or eaten in order to establish a salt covenant. For example, we see in the story of Elisha that he broke a curse over Jericho by pouring salt into the water source of the city.

Salt covenants with the true God are an important part of our commission. From a biblical perspective, salt covenants influence three important areas in our calling. First of all, we see that God entered into an everlasting salt covenant with His priests.

All the heave offerings of the holy things, which the children of Israel offer to the Lord, I have given to you and your sons and daughters with you as an ordinance forever; it is a covenant of salt forever before the Lord with you and your descendants with you (Numbers 18:19).

Second, we see that God entered into a salt covenant with kings.

Should you not know that the Lord God of Israel gave the dominion over Israel to David forever, to him and his sons, by a covenant of salt? (2 Chronicles 13:5)

And third we see that God entered into a salt covenant with the earth.

You are the salt of the earth; but if the salt loses its flavor, how shall it be seasoned? It is then good for nothing but to be thrown out and trampled underfoot by me (Matthew 5:13).

The two Scriptures from the Old Testament reflect eternal truths that we live in today and to which we have been called. The areas mentioned are three of the most important areas of our calling.

Being priests enables us to legally and effectively step into the gap for people. As kings, we can legally exercise the authority of Jesus Christ. As salt on the earth, we are God's ingredients so He can bring heaven on earth.

In this context, the fact that Jesus says we are the salt of the earth receives a much richer significance. On the one hand the earth or land was cleansed with salt. On the other hand Jesus referred to a salt covenant. Jesus started a new covenant on the earth. And because we are the salt of the earth, we are the covenant sign of it. Even more so because He has established us as covenant partners to spread the Kingdom of God here on the earth.

Now because we eat the salt of the king's palace and it is not proper for us to witness the king's discredit, therefore we send to inform the king, in order that a search may be made in the book of the records of your fathers, in which you will learn that this is a rebellious city, hurtful to kings and provinces, and that sedition was stirred up in it of old. That is why [it] was laid waste (Ezra 4:14-15 AMPC).

We see that eating the salt of the palace is a salt covenant between the king of Persia and the Samaritans during the time of the rebuilding of the temple.

Even though the favor and the word of the Lord confirmed to the Jews that it was right to rebuild the temple, the Samaritans referred to the salt covenant that they had with King Esarhaddon. On the foundation of this covenant they were even able to stop the building of the temple. The temple construction was interrupted for 16 years.

We can see what kind of power these covenants have—they can delay the promises of God. In how many areas of our lives do we have the impression that the fulfillment of a promise seems to take forever? This delay may even cause us to doubt the Word of God and His promise, because in spite of holding on by faith with all strength we see hardly any change.

There is a possibility that there is a salt covenant in our life that we are not aware of. It has been annulled by our baptism, so we can finally be released for our promise and run the race we have been called to by God our Father.

We resolve covenants and cleanse our bloodline through bloodline prayer so nothing can be in our way. This is how we can fulfill our Father's will as a holy priesthood, the fullness of our calling, and bring heaven to earth and release the Kingdom of God and His glory on earth.

CHAPTER 4

THE TESTIMONY OF MY BLOODLINE

Two chapters earlier I wrote about the covenant of God. I explained that we must align our lives and the pasts of our ancestors with the covenant of God. I would like to expand on the understanding of the transgression of our forefathers and why our repentance for their sin is so vital.

First, we need to understand what our bloodline reflects. Which information is anchored in our DNA? Or to be more explicit: Which testimony of our forefathers is still rooted in our blood that the accuser could use against us?

Let's have a look at the report about creation for this:

Then God said, "Let Us make man in Our image, according to Our likeness; let them have dominion over the fish of the sea, over the birds of the air, and over the cattle, over all the

earth and over every creeping thing that creeps on the earth."
So God created man in His own image; in the image of God
He created him; male and female He created them (Genesis
1:26-27).

The amazing thing about this account is that man is created in
the image and likeness of God. God created man in His image, in
His likeness. By creating man He put a crown on all of creation.
Man is the cream of the crop, the cherry on the whipped cream,
and the diamond among pebbles.

God was so delighted when He saw everything He created
on the sixth day that He exclaimed about His entire creation:
"It is very good!" At the end of every day God said that what He
created was good—except on the second day, which is not yet
relevant at this point. Through creation man not only completed
God's work, he became the climax at God's horizon. There is
nothing else that God created with such intimacy, nothing else
He dedicated Himself to as much as the creation of man.

God Himself became the prototype for the creation of man.
He used Himself as prototype because there was no source, no
pattern, and no imagination that would have been more amazing,
beautiful, majestic, and perfect than Him. This is the dedication
with which He brought forth man.

THE HEBREW WORD *DEMUTH*

The Hebrew word for "likeness" is *demuth*. The Hebrew language is a very picturesque language. This is why it can sometimes become difficult to translate the Hebrew text in our present-day languages. Words we use in English, for example, are a simple accumulation of letters without any meaning. Simply the fact that you put them together causes the letters to make sense.

The ancient Hebrew is completely different. Every letter derives from a pictogram—a little picture that has a meaning. Words are a combination of letters, and each individual letter contains a certain meaning. That is why when we receive a Hebrew word it is a composition of letters full of meaning.

A simple example to make it clear. The Hebrew word for "father" is *av*. It is composed of the letters *alef* and *bet*. *Alef* means "strong" or "leader," *bet* means "house" or "family." So the word for father implies the strong leader of a house or a family.

The letter *hei* describes the essence, substance, and the character of a thing. If we combine *hei* with the letters or the word for "father," *av*, we receive *ahav* which means the character, substance, or essence of a father or the strong leader of the house. What is the character of the father or the strong leader of the house? It is *ahav*, and *ahav* is the Hebrew word for love. Love is the character or essence of the Father. And the Bible says that God our Father is love.

This is a great example for the beauty of the Hebrew language. It explains also that the simple translation into English is more complex, because English is not a picturesque language. In order to reflect the Hebrew expressions in words, our translations are more descriptive. And in spite of all our efforts in translation it is difficult to reflect the entire content of even one of those words.

Let's return to the Hebrew word *demuth*. God uses *demuth* when creating man, and this is how He wants to bring across that he is created in God's image.

Demuth describes the similarity between two things in an alleviated way. However, it also means *reflection* or *replication*. Normally we would say that a replication is nothing special. But in this case it is different. Not only are we a replication of the most amazing being there is, but also it was God Himself who made us. It is from these facts that we can see that we have been created in a perfect way. And God Himself confirms it:

I will praise You, for I am fearfully and wonderfully made; marvelous are Your works, and that my soul knows very well (Psalms 139:14).

For You have made him a little lower than the angels, and You have crowned him with glory and honor (Psalms 8:5).

The Hebrew word that has been translated as "angels" here is *Elohim*. So "God" would have been a much more correct version of this word than "angel," but it could also mean angels. This Scripture expresses that man has been made a little lower than God. This makes sense because we are called to reveal God's manifold wisdom to the angels and not the other way round.

To the intent that now the manifold wisdom of God might be made known by the church to the principalities and powers in the heavenly places (Ephesians 3:10).

If we are a creation that is elevated above the angels, then it is our job to also reveal more about God to the angels and to open realms to them that they did not know to this point.

This may sound a bit wild, but it has to be the truth, because we have been made way more glorious than angels. Most Christians need to come to grips with this statement first because they consider the angels a little lower than God, but higher than man.

Angelic beings have no issue whatsoever with the fact that they have been made lower than man. They are simply waiting for us to live our creational status to the fullest extent. Doing this would mean glory and honor for angelic beings as well. This is why it is an honor for angels to submit to the service of God.

Are they not all ministering spirits sent forth to minister for those who will inherit salvation? (Hebrews 1:14)

I pray that we would come into the revelation, knowledge, and understanding of what it means to have been created in the image and likeness of God.

The root of *demuth* is *damah*, and many scholars consider *dam* as the root thereof. This is amazing in many ways and certainly a road sign for bloodline prayer, because *dam* is the Hebrew word for *blood*. Being created in the likeness of God also means that the blood of the first man came from Him. It is a clean, perfect, undefiled, glorious blood without sin. This blood reflected the glory of God, and if we had looked at its DNA we would not have found any defilement or sickness, fault, or decomposition.

This blood was so perfect that man would have lived eternally with his physical body. Not only that, the process of decomposition in his body would never have started and he would have forever remained in his perfect God-given state.

It is man's assignment to be fruitful and to multiply. Imagine Adam and Eve's descendants if they had not sinned. They would have been perfect beings with perfect blood and amazing DNA. Just like Adam we would all have reflected God in everything. We know, however, that things went differently. Man fell and sinned. The Fall started a new process—a process of death.

God had told man: If you eat from the tree of the knowledge of good and evil, you will die. The Bible says that life is in the blood.

For the life of the flesh is in the blood (Leviticus 17:11).

SIN, BLOOD, AND GENETIC MAKE-UP

If blood is connected to life and man initiated the process of dying, simple logic will tell you that something must have happened to man's blood. The blood that had been so perfect was stained and received a record of the Fall.

For the wages of sin is death (Romans 6:23).

Medical science speaks about DNA as the area where our genetic make-up is stored. Now that the Fall is recorded in the blood, this genetic make-up gets passed on from generation to generation. As I mentioned before, the descendants of man would have been just as perfect as the original couple. But because of the Fall things look completely different.

From this point on sin was passed on from one generation to the next generation. We know how the story continues: Cain and Abel were the immediate descendants, the next generation that came forth from Adam and Eve. Yet the problem was that sin in

Adam and Eve's blood was passed on to their descendants. And that is why a murder happened right in the very next generation. Out of jealousy Cain killed Abel. The question we must ask is: Where did this jealousy come from? At the beginning of mankind, there was no jealousy; it was unknown to man. The answer is that it was a direct result of the sin of Adam and Eve that Cain carried on the inside of him, inside his DNA. And sin developed its own dynamic. If sin does not get any boundaries, it becomes self-propelled.

MADE IN THE IMAGE OF GOD AND IN *HIS* LIKENESS

This is the book of the genealogy of Adam. In the day that God created man, He made him in the likeness of God. He created them male and female, and blessed them and called them Mankind in the day they were created. And Adam lived one hundred and thirty years, and begot a son in his own likeness, after his image, and named him Seth (Genesis 5:1).

From the chronology of the descendants of Adam we get amazing insight. The creation account tells us that man was made into the image and likeness of God. In Genesis 5:1, we read that Adam was created in the likeness of God. But look closely in whose image Adam begat his son Seth. Seth was not created in the image and likeness of God. He was begotten in the image and likeness of Adam!

Had Seth been created in the image and likeness of God, he would have been as perfect as his father in the beginning. He would have had the potential to live forever, and his blood would have had no trace of sin and death.

But Seth was begotten in the image and likeness of Adam, which means that everything Adam carried was passed on to his son or to the next generation after him as an inheritance.

And He has made from one blood every nation of men to dwell on all the face of the earth, and has determined their preappointed times and the boundaries of their dwellings (Acts 17:26).

In this verse in Acts, we see that we have all been made from one blood. The blood that flows in every single person today began with Adam. Each one of us carries the blood of Adam. Not only that, but we also carry the blood of our direct ancestors. Seth begat Enosh in his image and in his likeness. The name *Enosh* means "weak and feeble man." This means that whatever Adam had passed on to Seth, Seth passed on to Enosh, in addition to his own iniquity and blood. Subsequently Enosh passed his own sin on to his son Cainan and added to the iniquity of Seth and Adam. Cainan in turn added his own sins to the ones from Enosh, Seth, and Adam, and passed them on to his son Mahalalel.

We can continue in this train of thought all until we end up with our own blood, because we have all been begotten in the image and likeness of our physical father. We carry his DNA as well as his blood covenants. I recognize that clearly when I look at myself: If you see me, you recognize that I reflect my father. We have the same forehead, the same nose, the same hands, both of our little fingers are not straight, and there are many more things. But even more amazing in many ways is the fact that I have the manners of my dad. Sometimes I catch myself holding the steering wheel just the way he does. Or I realize the way I lie on my sofa is just the same way he lies on his. Even in these things I reflect my father. I am not aware of it; it is just simply a part of me. My father has passed those things on to me, because I was begotten in his image and likeness.

Sometimes as we pick up pictures of ancestors dating all the way back five, six, or seven generations, we recognize the similarity of facial expressions or other family characteristics. Or rather we should say that we find their characteristics in us. How very fascinating.

What we find many times as well are sicknesses and diseases that are stored in our genes. I have heard from some families how a specific form of cancer is passed on from one generation to the next. It goes much further than three or four generations. It is a bloodline problem that must be resolved.

We have heard stories from families who shared that for generations financial ruin occurred. Others report that their families keep experiencing similar blows or that a murder or a mysterious death happens in every other generation and that it has been going on for more than three or four generations. Many times, these are results of sin, iniquity, and covenants that can be traced to things from their ancestors that need to be dissolved from their bloodlines.

When we consider where our ancestors come from and what they did, we get an idea of the kinds of things our blood carries. Let me use my own life as an example: I am Croatian, and my ancestors come from Bosnia. The blood shed on our territory during the last centuries states what kind of things are in my bloodline.

Historical research conveys that Croatians originate from Iran. Some even go as far as to say that we originate from what is called Mongolia today. These are areas where an incredible number of altars were built, murders were committed, and blood covenants were cut.

PRESENT IN THE LOINS OF OUR ANCESTORS

You may think to yourself: But what does that have to do with me?

Even if it may sound unusual to you, allow me to explain it briefly from a spiritual point of view. To a certain extent you even participated in these activities. This may sound strange at first; however, we want to consider it from a biblical perspective.

Here mortal men receive tithes, but there he receives them, of whom it is witnessed that he lives. Even Levi, who receives tithes, paid tithes through Abraham, so to speak, for he was still in the loins of his father when Melchizedek met him (Hebrews 7:8-10).

Have a look at this Scripture. The Word says that Abraham gave Melchizedek the tithe, and at the same time Levi gave his tithe to Melchizedek. We would say that this is not possible, because he was not yet born or present; he was born four generations later. Yet from a spiritual point of view he was present in the loins of Abraham! This is why he could also participate in the blessing that this covenant brought forth.

For as in Adam all die, even so in Christ all shall be made alive (1 Corinthians 15:22).

So we see here how in one way each of us participated in the sin of Adam and our ancestors, which thus has become iniquity. We all originate from one blood—the blood of Adam. And because we were present in the loins of Adam, we all died in and through Adam.

But the glorious news is that even though we all died in Adam, we have the possibility to come alive in Christ again. In and through Christ we are alive, redeemed, justified, sanctified, cleansed, purified, lifted high, taken care of—we have been forgiven and we have risen to new life.

Please allow me to give you an example. Imagine that one of my ancestors would have died before having been able to have descendants. Under those circumstances I would not have come into the world. This allows us to conclude that I was somehow present in my ancestors. This is what the Bible describes when it speaks about being present in the loins of our forefathers.

As I wrote earlier, we have to understand that there are spiritual principles in our lives that on the one hand manifest immediately without any activation on our side. On the other hand there are also principles that are being released through Christ, but only manifested in our lives through our activation. This is one of the reasons why we fast, pray, praise, confess, and proclaim and so much more.

We can see that there are curses that have been in effect since Adam. For instance, we see that women who are saved, who fear God, who are full of love and full of the Holy Spirit, experience pain when giving birth. This pain clearly is a result of the Fall of the first man. Often diseases and suffering that godly people die from are the result of generational covenants, curses, and sins. And it happens even though Jesus has conquered everything already and we do not have to add anything to it.

This is exactly why bloodline prayer matters so much to us. There may be guilt in our bloodlines that will never hinder us in our personal lives—on the one hand because they have been erased through our salvation. On the other hand, it may be because the accuser has never presented them against us.

The more we go from glory to glory through Christ to spread the Kingdom of God, the more the accuser will make an effort to cause things in our bloodlines to accuse us before God. All of this happens to prevent the Kingdom of heaven coming to the earth.

The more authority you receive in the Kingdom of God, the more important it is for you to take care of your bloodline. At almost every level and elevation the enemy tries to go through your bloodline more intensely so that he can prevent the expansion of the Kingdom. He wants you to fall. Paul confirms this in regard to the office of the elders.

Not a novice, lest being puffed up with pride he fall into the same condemnation as the devil (1 Timothy 3:6).

(Note by translator: The German translation *Neue Genfer Übersetzung* translates: "That he should not get puffed up about his new position, and give the enemy the possibility to rightly accuse him.")

Here is our solution! Jesus Christ, His body, His blood, His cross, and His resurrection! There is nothing and nobody, no power and no voice that can overcome Jesus Christ. Because in Him everything was subjected until all eternity.

We have to actively use this in our bloodline prayer and position ourselves through it in the courts of heaven. So we can receive for our bloodline here and now what Jesus paid for and released 2,000 years ago.

For the wages of sin is death, but the gift of God is eternal life in Christ Jesus our Lord (Romans 6:23).

CHAPTER 5

IT'S ABOUT AUTHORITY, NOT ABOUT SALVATION

I want to make an important point that is often misunderstood in bloodline prayer—bloodline prayer is not necessary for our salvation.

There is no need to pray about your bloodline to receive salvation. Salvation is a result of your faith and your confession of your faith. The cleansing of our bloodline allows us to be placed in a position and authority that God desires for us to have— an authority and position we need to take for the sake of the Kingdom of God, to expand it here and now.

In the previous chapter, we talked about the blood and what kind of effects the blood has on our lives. The Hebrew word for "blood" is *dam*, and according to the *Theological Wordbook of the Old Testament*, *dam* (blood) or *dama*, which means "in God's likeness," guarantees that man is a faithful and adequate representative of God and His authority on earth.

We can also see that God has given the earth to man and that He told him to have dominion over it. We read that man gave names to the animals and that creation accepted man's dominion. But the moment sin came into people's life and their blood was defiled, he lost authority on the earth.

The ground was cursed as a consequence, and it became a plight for Adam to till the ground, because now it brought forth thorns and thistles. From this time forth the earth no longer reacted the same way to Adam's authority, but to the sin he had committed and to the curse that was released on creation. This developed into a decrease of Adam's authority.

Then to Adam He said, "Because you have heeded the voice of your wife, and have eaten from the tree of which I commanded you, saying, 'You shall not eat of it': Cursed is the ground for your sake; in toil you shall eat of it all the days of your life. Both thorns and thistles it shall bring forth for you, and you shall eat the herb of the field" (Genesis 3:17-18).

Authority is something that has been given to us up to a certain degree, but if we want to increase our authority we have to grow into it. God wants each one of us to live up to the full potential of the authority we are called to. Yet many times we may be called to something, and in spite of our passion and love for God we never reach it. One of the reasons could be that the enemy still has legal rights in your life that allow the accuser to hold you back from your destiny.

THE HEBREW WORD AVON

The record of Joshua being clothed in new garments allows interesting insight into the spiritual world to us. This can help us to understand even more about the necessity for cleansing.

Then he showed me Joshua the high priest standing before the Angel of the Lord, and Satan standing at his right hand to oppose him. And the Lord said to Satan, "The Lord rebuke you, Satan! The Lord who has chosen Jerusalem rebuke you! Is this not a brand plucked from the fire?" Now Joshua was clothed with filthy garments, and was standing before the Angel.

Then He answered and spoke to those who stood before Him, saying, "Take away the filthy garments from him." And to him He said, "See, I have removed your iniquity from you, and I will clothe you with rich robes" (Zechariah 3:1-4).

Satan brought forth legitimate accusations against the high priest Joshua. This is amazing because the high priest sanctifies himself 364 days of the year to step into the Holy of Holies on that special day of the year. This means that his entire life was aligned to the focus of being sanctified and purified for that moment when he would stand before God.

In spite of his efforts and the cleansing he went through, satan could still come before God with accusations against him.

These accusations did not necessarily originate in his own life. The Bible speaks about iniquity that had to be taken away from him. The Hebrew word for iniquity is *avon*. *Avon* can be translated in several different ways—guilt, injustice, rebellion, trespassing, and sin are some of them. *Avon*, however, does not only stand for sin. There are different Hebrew words that are used for sin. For example, *chata*, a terminology expressing the fact that a specific sin is committed. The sum of all those individual sins evoked remaining consequences, which is then called *avon* and translated as "iniquity."

Thus, iniquity is the result of a lifestyle of sin. Psalms 38:5 says that iniquity pushes people down because of its heavy weight. Psalms 65:4 even states that iniquity is stronger than man and therefore can generate a noxious destiny, even to the point that destruction becomes inevitable (see Ps. 104:43)

Sins frequently mentioned as being related to iniquity are idolatry, the shedding of blood, violence, sexual impurity, perversion, recklessness in regard to the poor, abuse of prophetic utterance, and trespassing godly laws. The sum total of the concept is—it is our iniquity that hinders us from living in our full predestined authority.

We see that the high priest Joshua wore dirty clothes. Please note that in the natural he wore very beautiful clothes. The garment of the high priest was a fashion designer artwork that caused everybody to marvel. The filthiness was what Joshua wore in the spirit. We can look stunning in the natural and yet what we look like before God is what truly matters.

You may be able to overlook many things in the natural. You can smile at someone or even laugh with that person, even though you have a grudge against them in your heart. You can share uplifting words with someone yet be mad at them in your heart. Although we can override so many things in the natural, things are very different in the spirit. The iniquity in our lives that has not been confessed is known in the spirit world in the same way it was with the high priest Joshua. It is attached to us like filthy garments.

I even want to go so far as to state that we ridicule ourselves when we put up a mask in the natural with our heads raised high pretending that everything is fine, even though we carry filthy garments in the spiritual world. We do not want to be ridiculous; we want to be pleasing vessels unto God. And this is God's desire as well. However, it requires humility, because so many times we have to humble ourselves before God, often even before man, to give the Lord the opportunity to raise us up and exchange our filthy clothes.

I acknowledged my sin to You, and my iniquity I have not hidden. I said, "I will confess my transgressions to the Lord," and You forgave the iniquity of my sin. Selah (Psalms 32:5).

Humbling ourselves starts with repentance and reversal. The next step is to bring the fruit of that repentance in agreement with our repentance.

When the high priest experienced the described exchange of his clothes, his position of authority was changed. At the same time the angel of the Lord reminded him that his lifestyle needed to be in alignment with this swap. He reminded him about walking in the ways of the Lord.

Then the Angel of the Lord admonished Joshua, saying, "Thus says the Lord of hosts: 'If you will walk in My ways, and if you will keep My command, then you shall also judge My house, and likewise have charge of My courts; I will give you places to walk among these who stand here'" (Zechariah 3:6-7).

When iniquity was wiped out, God gave him access to a greater measure of authority. The iniquity that the high priest Joshua had been burdened with may have come from his own trespassing, but certainly also from his ancestors.

THE ACCUMULATION OF INIQUITY

But in the fourth generation they shall return here, for the iniquity of the Amorites is not yet complete (Genesis 15:15).

We can read and learn a few things from this Scripture. The context here is that God had revealed to Abraham that the land he was standing on was given to him as his property because Abraham had entered into a covenant with God. However, Abraham could not immediately take this land as his possession. Only his descendants would return there and take this land as their possession about 470 years later (they spent 430 years in Egypt and 40 years in the desert).

It is amazing, though, that God said that the iniquity of the Amorites was not yet complete. This means that the Amorites had legitimate rights and authority in regard to this land. Through his provision God told Abraham that this right of the Amorites would expire around 400 years later because of their accumulation of iniquity. So first of all we see that iniquity can cause legal rights to terminate.

To this day this has not changed. The Word of God says that all things are possible to him who believes and that God will give us everything we ask for. What a tremendous promise. It is important to stand on this promise—it is our right. Yet, at the same time God warns us:

Husbands, likewise, dwell with them with understanding, giving honor to the wife, as to the weaker vessel, and as being heirs together of the grace of life, that your prayers may not be hindered (1 Peter 3:7).

REDEEMING *your* BLOODLINE

Even if we have a right to the promises of God, positioning ourselves in the wrong way and having iniquity in our lives can disqualify us from receiving them. They won't have any effect on our lives.

Thus a God-fearing, God-loving, Bible-reading, tongue-talking, signs-and-wonders-working intercessor, and evangelist can give the enemy access to his life, hindering his prayers by the way he treats his wife. You can quote the Bible in your life forward and backward, but if the enemy has any legal rights in your life he can sap your authority.

To avoid any kind of misunderstanding, I want to mention that naturally the same applies for God-fearing, wonderfully made women of God.

God has given us commandments that are a blessing to us. But if we do not align ourselves to them, it can cause a lot of frustration because we do not see the effects of the authority God intended for us to have. This is the reason why we want to humble and submit ourselves under the mighty hand of God—so He can lift us up in the presence of our enemies. May the enemy find no rights that will allow him to stop or hinder the expansion of the Kingdom of God that is supposed to happen through us.

Second, we learn that iniquity remains and can pile up from generation to generation. Genesis 15:16 explains that iniquity is the accumulation of sin over generations that can have an effect on our lives. We do not know exactly how long the Amorites had accumulated their iniquity, yet we can be certain that it had already happened for several generations. At that time there were not many people who feared God; even fewer people groups feared God. But we know that their guilt was piled up for at least another 400 years. To sum it all up, Scripture teaches us that iniquity can pile up over more than three or four generations and have an effect on our lives. This is the reason why we see Ezra, Nehemiah, and Daniel asking for forgiveness—for themselves, for Israel, and for their forefathers.

Since the days of our fathers to this day we have been very guilty, and for our iniquities we, our kings, and our priests have been delivered into the hand of the kings of the lands, to the sword, to captivity, to plunder, and to humiliation, as it is this day (Ezra 9:8).

Then those of Israelite lineage separated themselves from all foreigners; and they stood and confessed their sins and the iniquities of their fathers (Nehemiah 9:2).

Third, we understand that iniquity will not always be avenged immediately. Even though the Amorites had already been guilty, it took several generations more until this iniquity had full effect in the natural.

If we do not remove iniquity, it has a certain potential to limit us. It can cut us off from authority and blessings. The Bible says in First Peter 5:8 that our adversary, the devil, walks around like a roaring lion seeking whom he may devour. Revelation 12:10 tells us that the accuser accuses us before God day and night. We see that the devil constantly seeks something that would hinder God the righteous judge from working through us and on our behalf. I am convinced that the more we grow in authority, the more dangerous we become for the devil. That's why things in our bloodline that have not been searched out before now suddenly become relevant.

PRESIDENTIAL ELECTION

This process can be compared to a political career. Imagine, for example, the presidential election in the United States. The candidates who run for office have to have a thick skin. During their entire campaign the opponent constantly and without any interruption looks for things that might discredit the other candidate. Even the candidate's family tree is being searched to find a scandal among their ancestors. Every minor thing suddenly gets turned into a scandal, even though no one ever cared about it before—at least the majority of people. All of this effort is made simply to prove that this candidate is not a good choice. Many reproaches can be taken without any comment, yet serious accusations need to be answered. They need to be confirmed or denied. In some cases, a public apology or statement is required.

This is a fitting comparison to show how things can move in the spiritual realm. The higher you move in spiritual and natural authority, the greater the probability that you have to receive a cleansing from the iniquity that you or your ancestors have caused.

Many times we notice that opposition increases when promotion comes our way. "New level, new devil" is a saying English-speaking preachers like to use. It means that with every ascent you bump into new demons. The more you ascend, the more you have to cleanse and purify your life. But the spiritual world does not only release demons against you. At the same time, there is also a release of new angels for you for this new level to serve and support you. They help us to exercise government in the positions that we have come into.

The lives of spiritual leaders can help in an amazing way. Leaders who had difficulties in certain areas in their lives that they were never able to remove—after a certain time the accuser caused them to fall. These things surfaced when the specific leader started to get public elevation. At that point the enemy used the opportunity to reveal the iniquity and make the damage as big as possible for the Body of Christ.

This confirms again that iniquity is not always punished immediately. One of the reasons, of course, is the surpassing greatness of God's' grace (see Ps. 102:10-11). On the other hand, it is because the accuser and the powers of darkness are waiting for the right moment to make us stumble. That way they can make the Body of Christ appear to be untrustworthy.

As we take care of our bloodlines, iniquity, altars, covenants, and blood shed of our ancestors, we need to understand that we are inevitably moving within in the courts of heaven.

COURTS OF HEAVEN

During the course of this book, I have already mentioned the courts of heaven several times. This expression may be unusual or new to you. I will not go into the depth of this subject here, but I want to lay a quick foundation about the understanding of the courts of heaven. In case you would like to learn more about it, I recommend that you read the books of our friend Robert Henderson—*Operating in the Courts of Heaven.*

Most people never give prayer much reflection. Usually they just pray the Lord's Prayer whenever they need something from the Lord. They consider God as their Father and hope that God will hear them. The best-case scenario is that they believe He does.

God is not just our Father; He is also a King who has a Kingdom. In addition to this He is a friend, He is Lord, but He also is the Judge in His courts in heaven.

For the Lord is our Judge, the Lord is our Lawgiver, the Lord is our King; he will save us (Isaiah 33:22).

This is probably one of my favorite Scriptures speaking about God being our Judge. God is a Judge to save and not to condemn. Normally people are afraid when they think about judgment or about God being a Judge because they are afraid He might decide something bad and they could be the ones suffering the consequences. But having God as our Judge is one of the most wonderful things we could possibly imagine. The Bible says here that God is our Lord, Judge, and lawgiver, followed by this great revelation: *He will save us!*

Every time I think about it, I am so delighted and I get goosebumps. God is Judge because He wants to save us, not to condemn us! The purpose of His laws, commandments, and righteousness is to save us and to judge on our behalf. You have to take a moment and think about how amazing this is.

Imagine you have a father who is a judge. As a child you have free access to your father and there are hardly any boundaries that would hinder you. The relationship to the father is often relaxed without major restrictions.

But if your father steps into his office as a judge, things look different. Even though he is your father, different protocols and regulations apply. If you don't stick to them you may be reprimanded or even thrown out. Does that mean that your father doesn't love you? Of course not! Yet different regulations are in effect in this context and you need to stick to them.

It is the same in the supernatural realm. When we pray and step into the courts of heaven, we have to stick to the regulations that apply there if we want to be successful.

Where can we find a confirmation in Scripture of the fact that there is a court in heaven, a courtroom, or even several courtrooms? When you look at the Bible you can see that it is full of legal language, painting a picture of court rooms with everything else included. We see, for example, that God is a Judge, Jesus is our lawyer, and the Holy Spirit is our advocate (see Isa. 33:22; 1 John 2:1; John 14:16). The foundations of His throne are righteousness and justice and there is a throne of grace—a place where grace rather than judgment is being released (see Ps. 89:15; Heb. 4:16). The Greek term translated "church" is *ekklesia*, which also is a legal term (see 1 Tim. 3:15). There is Jesus who acts as mediator and man of confidence (see 1 Tim 2:5). We also see witnesses—the so-called "cloud of witnesses" (see Heb. 12:1). The Bible speaks about the council of God, the courtroom itself, and the books of judgment that are being opened (see Jer. 23:18,22; Dan. 7:10). The devil appears as accuser and presents the accusations (see Rev. 12:10; 1 Tim 3:6). There are also ordinances written against us (see Col. 2:14). Scripture describes a process in court, and at the end a verdict is being executed, which starts with us the Church (see Ps. 82; 1 Pet. 4:17). This is only a short list to show how real and important our understanding about the courts of heaven is and how this arrangement can be found in the entire Bible.

God is a King with a Kingdom, which has rules and regulations, so it makes sense that God also has a judicial system in place for this. In the above list we do not see the accused person—this is where we come in. When we do bloodline prayers, we answer legal accusations of Satan, because otherwise they are being used against us.

As a counter-maneuver we can also summon the devil to court so that, through God, his dealings will come to an end. But this is the next step after bloodline prayer and not part of the teaching of this book.

Whenever we deal with regions, territories, nations, principalities, and powers in the heavenly places, we have to step into the courts of heaven. It is the only place where we can summon, claim, and overcome powers of darkness in the heavenly realm. Even Jesus had to step into a courtroom when He claimed nations for Himself after His resurrection.

I watched till thrones were put in place, and the Ancient of Days was seated; His garment was white as snow, and the hair of His head was like pure wool. His throne was a fiery flame, its wheels a burning fire; a fiery stream issued and came forth from before Him. A thousand thousands ministered to Him; ten thousand times ten thousand stood before Him. The court was seated, and the books were opened. I was watching in the night visions, and behold, One like the Son of Man, coming with the clouds of heaven!

He came to the Ancient of Days, and they brought Him near before Him. Then to Him was given dominion and glory and a kingdom, that all peoples, nations, and languages should serve Him. His dominion is an everlasting dominion, which shall not pass away, and His kingdom the one which shall not be destroyed (Daniel 7:9-10,13-14).

Revelations help us to become more effective, and our understanding of the courts of heaven helps us to be more successful in court.

I am convinced that many of us have been active in court without being aware of it because we trusted and followed the leading of the Holy Spirit in our prayers. In our lives we also do many things right without knowing how they function, yet if we get understanding we become more secure, more effective, and more protected. It is the same way with all revelations of God, including understanding the courts of heaven.

In bloodline prayer we enter the courts of heaven to respond to accusations against us by repenting and receiving forgiveness. At the same time, it is also part of protocol to know how to enter the courts and how to act and behave there. In this Scripture, you see how we present ourselves there:

But you have come to Mount Zion and to the city of the living God, the heavenly Jerusalem, to an innumerable company of angels, to the general assembly and church of the firstborn who are registered in heaven, to God the Judge of all, to the spirits of just men made perfect, to Jesus the Mediator of the new covenant, and to the blood of sprinkling that speaks better things than that of Abel (Hebrews 12:22-24).

So we come to the Holy Spirit, who is our Helper; to a general assembly; and also to the church of the firstborn, the judge of all, and the spirits of just men made perfect. We come to Jesus, the mediator of the new covenant and the blood of the sprinkling that speaks better things than that of Abel. But we have to be prepared so that a successful verdict can be spoken on our behalf.

Hebrews 4:16 shares with us that we have to step before the throne of God with boldness so we can receive grace and mercy in a times of need. Many times people tell me that they can step before the throne of grace anytime without any conditions. But this is not entirely correct. The throne of grace is a description of the Ark of the Covenant in the tent of meeting and the temple.

In Hebrew, the throne of grace is the mercy seat in the tabernacle; the Hebrew word is *kapporeth* and the root of this word is *kaphar*, meaning repentance and atonement. So if we step before the throne of grace boldly, we do so because we prepared ourselves through repentance; we do not go there emptyhanded. It is with repentance and atonement that we approach God, the righteous Judge of all, to receive grace and mercy in a time of need.

Many times He delivered them; but they rebelled in their counsel, and were brought low for their iniquity. Nevertheless He regarded their affliction, when He heard their cry; and for their sake He remembered His covenant, and relented according to the multitude of His mercies. He also made them to be pitied by all those who carried them away captive (Psalms 106:43-48).

This is why it is important that we have a heart that is ready to repent in case we have moved away from the order of God. Because this is how the grace of God overflows in our lives.

The next chapter will go into more detail about the requirements for successful bloodline prayer.

CHAPTER 6

REQUIREMENTS FOR SUCCESSFUL BLOODLINE PRAYER

Having acquired the understanding of the previous chapters, the following verse may be perceived in a very different way.

Ye have not yet resisted unto blood, striving against sin (Hebrews 12:4 ASV).

This Scripture can be taken literally through the revelations given in the previous chapters, because in bloodline prayer we declare war and strive against sin unto the blood. We release the redemption of Jesus Christ in our blood and our DNA because they still contain record of iniquity and false covenants all the way back to Adam.

It is our experience that a few requirements need to be fulfilled so that we can successfully receive the redemption for our bloodline. The following points are things that are regularly presented in the courts of heaven by the accuser. In case we do not meet the requirements, the entire process comes to a halt. Consequently, God cannot release a verdict on our behalf, even though He desires to do so.

In those cases, the result is not dependent on the power of God but on the fact that we did not meet the requirements. God created orders and protocols that allow Him to bless us when we stick to them.

Orders and protocols are spiritual laws such as "the wages of sin is death." This is a universal law that God established. The consequence of this law is that God cannot reward sin with blessing, no matter how much He would like to reward us. If we have sin in our lives and allow it, we inhibit God from blessing us.

The following requirements should be met as spiritual law and foundation:

SALVATION

First of all you should be able to positively answer the question: Do you believe in God the Father, Jesus Christ His Son, and the Holy Spirit and that there is no other God but Him?

But as many as received him, to them gave he the right to become children of God, even to them that believe on his name: who were born, not of blood, nor of the will of the flesh, nor of the will of man, but of God (John 1:12-13).

Being born again is the core foundation of going to war victoriously against the enemy and against iniquity in our lives. God does not allow any other gods besides Him. Not because He is egoistic, but because He does not want His greatness to be debased, just as He does not want in regard to His love, grace, mercy, power, might, glory, and righteousness. Because he is the one and only God and all others are liars. This is also the first of the Ten Commandments:

I am the Lord your God, who brought you out of the land of Egypt, out of the house of bondage. You shall have no other gods before Me (Exodus 20:2-3).

In John 1:12-13, we see why being born again is so important. I have written about the blood a bit more extensively. Being born again confirms to us that we are not primarily made from natural blood, but we were born of God. We have then become a new creation; old things have gone and new things have started.

Through our salvation we laid our corner stone. It is the prerequisite to no longer be judged according to our flesh and adamic blood, which is full of iniquity and negative covenants, but according to the new creation in Jesus Christ.

Having been born again, not of corruptible seed but incorruptible, through the word of God which lives and abides forever (1 Peter 1:23).

In case you have not received Jesus Christ in your life yet, but you would like to decide to live a life with this wonderful King, you can do that using the following prayer. Pray out loud:

Gracious Father, I come before You as a sinner who needs salvation and redemption. I ask Your forgiveness for my sins and my ungodly lifestyle. I have come to believe that You have sent Your Son, Jesus Christ, who died on the cross and rose again after three days, to save me. I believe that salvation doesn't come any other way but through Jesus Christ alone. Jesus, I open my heart to You and I ask You to dwell in it and to become the Lord of my life. Holy Spirit, I invite you to lead and guide me to live a godly, holy, and sanctified life in peace and joy. Father, I thank You that You are in my heart now and that I am Your child. Amen.

BAPTISM

Were you baptized after you purposefully decided to believe in Jesus? Baptism is another step and requirement to lead a successful Christian life.

Salvation causes us to be born again—old things have passed away. When we get baptized after intentionally deciding for it, we bury the old life in the death of Jesus and get a resurrection in the life of Jesus Christ. Because covenants can only be resolved by death, baptism is not only a confirmation or a symbol of your salvation, it is essential so we can walk in the newness of life.

I have mentioned above that God created man in His image and likeness, but all following generations were begotten in the image and likeness of their forefathers. As this is the case, it is important to return to the first state of creation.

Therefore we were buried with Him through baptism into death, that just as Christ was raised from the dead by the glory of the Father, even so we also should walk in newness of life. For if we have been united together in the likeness of His death, certainly we also shall be in the likeness of His resurrection (Romans 6:4-5).

Do not lie to one another, since you have put off the old man with his deeds, and have put on the new man who is renewed in knowledge according to the image of Him who created him (Colossians 3:9-10).

The word for "likeness" in Romans 6:5 is the Greek word *homoioma*. This expression is used in the Septuagint in Genesis 1:26 for the expression of "likeness." This also applies for the word "image" in Colossians 3:10. Both Scriptures confirm that we are being returned into the original state by baptism, being made into the likeness and image of God.

Personally, I do not know another instruction that God has given us for this but baptism. Baptism is not just a symbol; it is a powerful blessing from God to release power and creational order in our lives. Baptism withdraws the right of the accuser to accuse us with our past and the iniquity in our bloodlines. However, in some areas we have to actively enforce this through bloodline prayer.

REPENTANCE AND FORGIVENESS

Are you ready to repent and to receive forgiveness? I already mentioned a few things about the throne of grace earlier on.

Let us therefore come boldly to the throne of grace, that we may obtain mercy and find grace to help in time of need (Hebrews 4:16).

What a wonderful call. We have unlimited access to the throne of grace, to find grace and help in time of need.

As I previously stated, the throne of grace is a term that comes from the Old Testament and describes the Ark of the Covenant in the Holy of Holies. It is the Hebrew word *kapporeth. Kapporeth* is derived from the root word *kaphar*, which means "atonement or repentance." So if we boldly come before the throne of grace, we do not come empty-handed. We come with repentance and a heart ready to repent. It is a reflection of greatness and strength to be able to ask God and man for forgiveness. There is a lot of truth in the saying that we should not trust nor follow a person who cannot admit their own mistakes or ask for forgiveness.

The Greek word for repentance is *metanoia*, and it describes the process of a change of mind or turning to the opposite direction. It means that we have to decide for a lifestyle of repentance. This does not mean that we mainly confess our sins, but that we are adapting a lifestyle in which we align ourselves with the will of God.

FORGIVING OTHERS

Are you prepared to forgive other people?

Give us this day our daily bread. And forgive us our debts, as we forgive our debtors. And do not lead us into temptation, but deliver us from the evil one. For Yours is the kingdom and the power and the glory forever. Amen (Matthew 6:11-13).

This Scripture is an excerpt of the best known and possibly most often quoted prayer of all time. It is called the Lord's Prayer. What a tremendous asset and treasure it is! Tertullian, one of the church fathers from the second century, rightly said that the entire Gospel is summed up in it. It is so clear that its message even makes sense to children. But it is also so deep that it brings the greatest teachers of the Bible to reverence and awe.

One of the messages it contains is that our sin should be forgiven just as we forgive our debtors. This binds us to forgiveness.

You need to live a lifestyle of forgiveness. Be like your heavenly Father, who is slow to anger and great in mercy and forgiveness. In my opinion this is one of the foundational premises to protect us from every root of bitterness that would like to sprout and become a stumbling stone to us.

PRIORITY: THE KINGDOM OF GOD

Are you ready to give up things for the Kingdom of God? Jesus lived a life of self-sacrifice; He has exemplified this way of life for us. We have been called to live the same kind of lifestyle because the Word of God says that to give is more blessed than to receive.

It may be your perception that things are taken away from you when you give them up. But the opposite is the case. Whenever God requires something from us it is merely because He has greater foresight than us. He sees blessings in front of us that we cannot recognize ourselves. But He wants to prepare us for them and make sure that we will indeed receive them.

But seek first the kingdom of God and His righteousness, and all these things shall be added to you (Matthew 6:33).

The principles in the Kingdom of God frequently are the complete opposite of natural principles. In the Kingdom of

God, we lose our lives to gain them. We give to become rich. We humble ourselves to be elevated. We serve to win greatness. The last will be the first and the first will be the last.

We see that we should not be blinded by the natural world. Make the Kingdom of God your priority and you will experience love, blessing, and favor in a way you could have never imagined before.

PART OF THE BODY OF CHRIST

Are you part of a larger Body of Christ in your area or are you a part of a church or an ekklesia? The church or the ekklesia is the greatest legal power on the earth, but it appears that she still doesn't know that about herself. On the other hand, Christians do not believe in being part in it, and this is where being blinded starts.

In the Old Testament, we see that the anointing of a person can be transferred to another individual. The anointing of priests, kings, prophets, judges, patriarchs, leaders of armies, etc. was transferred from one individual to another. From Elijah to Elisha, from Moses to Joshua, from David to Solomon, etc. But since the time of Jesus the anointing was no longer passed on to individuals only but also to assemblies and groups. We do not have just one prophet; we have many prophets. There is not just one son of God; there are many children of God. We have more than just one person ruling as king; we have all been called to kingship.

God calls us to be part of something collective. It means that we cannot merely be a part of the global Body of Christ. No, we have to actively participate in a local body of believers and live in fellowship with each other. And if we do so, Scripture tells us that we live in the light and the blood of Jesus cleanses us from all sin.

But if we walk in the light as He is in the light, we have fellowship with one another, and the blood of Jesus Christ His Son cleanses us from all sin (1 John 1:7).

We can see from this Scripture why it is so important to have vigorous fellowship with the local Body of Christ. Because by doing it we position ourselves in a way that the blood of Jesus can come to the full extent of its power and effect in our lives.

In case you do not belong to an ekklesia or to a church yet, decide to find one. And do not give room to that illusion that you will find a perfect church, because wherever human beings are involved, there will be shortcomings.

There are a few basic elements you should find in a church: Friendly interaction with each other, forgiveness, powerful teaching of the Word of God and biblical principles for daily living, the moving of the Holy Spirit, a striving for the gifts of the Holy Spirit, faith in signs and miracles, holiness, and sanctification, to simply list a few.

FINANCES

Are you a tither? Do you believe that your finances and your welfare are meant for your own provision but also for the provision of the Kingdom of God?

This book does not provide the right setting to discuss the teaching about tithing. However, I would like to mention that I am deeply convinced about the extraordinary importance of the tithe. We have seen in the courts of heaven that people's conscious decisions against tithing have become accusations against them numerous times.

Everything we do should be done by faith, not as a method. The same applies to giving the tithe—it has to be given by faith. In my opinion, churches should not ask their members to tithe arguing that their expenses need to be covered. We have to understand that the tithe that is given to the church has the purpose to be a blessing for the believer. It is wrong to put people under pressure in regard to tithing or to blame them for a lack of faith if they do not give it. But on the other hand, we should not shrink back from teaching about the overflowing blessing that comes from tithing, only because we are afraid we might offend someone or we do not want anyone to feel pressured. It is our job to strengthen and build up faith so people will start to walk according to those God-given principles. That is how the fruit and blessing will be visible in your personal life. I am convinced that it is impossible to walk in agreement with the principles of God without seeing the fruit thereof in the long run.

Do not lay up for yourselves treasures on earth, where moth and rust destroy and where thieves break in and steal; but lay up for yourselves treasures in heaven, where neither moth nor rust destroys and where thieves do not break in and steal. For where your treasure is, there your heart will be also (Matthew 6:19).

Where our treasure is that is where our heart is. Our heart testifies about what matters to us. We can recognize what is important to us by watching where our money is spent.

The heart works like a pump in our body and causes constant circulation of blood. Our blood carries stored information going back all the way to Adam, and this information influences our being because life is in the blood. Proverbs 23:7 confirms this: "For as he thinks in his heart, so is he."

How do you see your finances? Do you see them as your property and nobody is allowed to intervene, or do you consider them as God's property and you are simply the steward thereof?

Finances and the prosperity we enjoy have a purpose, if we pursue it. We use finances and treasures in agreement with God's mandate. Jesus says in Mark 10:29-30 that the things that we have given up for the sake of the Gospel will be returned to us a hundredfold in this time.

Of course God's wisdom for finances is greater than ours. If we steward them according to His will, we will not miss out, but we will enjoy them and also pass them on to our children's children.

Decide anew today to bring your finances in alignment. Ask God to provide the faith you need for it. And always keep in mind that God does not want to take anything away from you. He only desires to adjust our course so we can come into the pleasure of receiving a hundredfold (in this present time and age).

When we align our finances and our treasures according to the Kingdom of God, we position ourselves with a good testimony for the cleansing of our bloodline. At the same time we make room to see God step in as a witness in our favor speedily (see Mal. 3:3-5). Is there anyone else you'd rather have as a speedy witness than our gracious God and Judge?

CHAPTER 7

CONCLUSION

Before we start with the practical part of this book, I would like to mention one more thing: The prayers that you find in the coming chapters are a great way to start and are a result of years of experience in this area. But they do not provide a thorough cleansing of every individual bloodline. Our lives are too different for this.

Consider it more like beginning to walk down a path that leads us more and more into the kind of authority and freedom that are needed for every phase of our live. The higher we climb the ladder of authority, the more drastically the accuser will try to stop us, limit us, or shame us.

As mentioned before, if a person in the natural applies for the position of a minister, chancellor, or president, the life of this person will be searched through in almost every detail; hardly anything of relevance is hidden from the public. But not only is the personal life of this person searched through, but also the lives of their ancestors become of great interest. Should the grandfather have been in the SS, the question will be asked publicly whether this person should be allowed to have this position of authority at all. Even though the candidate is not part of the SS, they have to publicly renounce the conviction of their grandfather in order to persuade the public. Not only should he renounce the position of his grandfather, but it is even desired that he speaks against it publicly and declare himself to be just the very opposite of that.

We have experienced similar things in Germany. People striving for or getting into higher levels of authority have been searched through more thoroughly than before. Plagiarism is a fitting example. The doctoral theses of many German ministers were searched through to see if they contained anything copied or if any plagiarism could be found. For some this turned into a stumbling stone that caused them to lose their doctorate, but beyond that public pressure caused them to resign from their position. Not to mention the damage to their personal reputation. If they had not aspired to a higher level of authority, those unpleasant situations would never have happened.

That exact same principle applies for spiritual authority. The higher we climb in the area of spiritual authority, the greater the interest of the accuser to search through our lives. Because the higher we move up, the more dangerous it becomes for him.

This is why Revelation 12:10 says that we have an accuser who accuses us day and night before God. But in the following verse, we see the outstanding power of the awesome Word of God with which we can make the enemy hush.

And they overcame him by the blood of the Lamb and by the word of their testimony, and they did not love their lives to the death (Revelation 12:11).

So let us now take the next step and with the blood of the Lamb and the word of our testimony let us not love our lives more than our God and Redeemer.

Together with our Helper, the Holy Spirit, and our Lawyer, Jesus Christ, we want to stand before the one and only God, the righteous Judge, to redeem our bloodline.

For the glory and praise of the creator of heaven and earth!

CHAPTER 8

THE COURTS OF HEAVEN

Robert Henderson

I realize in this day of varying viewpoints on generational curses, sins of forefathers, and bloodline cleansing that the topic of dealing with the past and people's ancestral history can be a volatile subject. As someone once declared, however, "Someone with an experience is not at the mercy of someone with an argument." This has happened to me. I'm not saying I don't have a theological foundation for what I believe. I am saying, however, that I don't *just* have this. I have proven this concept in my own life and seen it proven in the lives of many others. Much like David refused to wear the armor of Saul because it didn't fit him and he had not proven it, so should we be as well. First Samuel 17:39 chronicles David as he was preparing to defeat the giant Goliath, dismissing the use of that which he had not tested or had experience with.

> *David fastened his sword to his armor and tried to walk, for he had not tested them. And David said to Saul, "I cannot walk with these, for I have not tested them." So David took them off.*

The last thing one would want is to go into battle with something you aren't confident in using. The battlefield is not the place to learn to use your equipment. That is a surefire way to become a casualty. The use of your weaponry has to be second nature to you by the time you get to the battlefield. David had no history with the armor of Saul. He did, however, know how to use a sling and stones. Of course we know from this famous story that this is exactly what happened. The apostle Paul tells us in Second Corinthians 10:4 that God has granted us weaponry to destroy the strongholds the devil uses to hold ground he has taken.

For the weapons of our warfare are not carnal but mighty in God for pulling down strongholds.

The cleansing of the bloodline of iniquitous history is one of the most powerful pieces of our arsenal that we have. If you can undo the legal right of the devil that he has derived from your ancestral lineage, much if not all the conflict you find yourself in can be stopped. This is what I have tested and proven to be real, theologically sound, and effective in securing and maintaining breakthrough. Again the apostle Paul tells Timothy in Second Timothy 2:6 as a young minister that he should only teach and give what he has proven in his own life.

The hardworking farmer must be first to partake of the crops.

In other words, we shouldn't try to just give principles to people; we should have tested them out on ourselves first. We must have *eaten* what we are giving to others to *eat*. We must know that what we have produced is good through having seen it work in our own lives. This has definitely happened in my life and the life of my family. It is still happening until this day. Anytime there is a problem that arises I consider whether it has its roots in an ancestral issue or not. It doesn't always, but quite often it does. When I discern and deal with something that is being empowered from the bloodline, there is almost always an immediate result.

Even as I am writing this I have just returned from Europe. Something occurred there that illustrates what I am saying. As I was ministering in a church there, a lady on the leadership team began to tell me about a young man who had become sexually active at seven years old. Even before she continued the story I knew this was a bloodline issue. Naturally speaking, a seven-year-old will not have an interest in the sexual things this young man had been involved in. She continued to reveal that this young man, now 17 years old, was tormented and had come for help. They had prayed with him and nothing had changed.

She said the people who were praying for him had declared it done and completed even though the young man by his own admission was still bound. They did this because they didn't want to admit defeat and didn't know what else to do. She asked if I could pray with him. I agreed but told her I only had a short time after the service.

They took me with the young man to a private office after the service. When I met the young man, his head hung in shame; his face showed oppression and perhaps even apprehension at what was about to happen. I assured him that there were only good intentions involved. We began to pray. I led him through a prayer of repentance for himself. I then led him in a prayer of repentance over his bloodline. He repented on behalf of his family and ancestry for any and all involvement with sexual and immoral behavior. I then took authority over the devil and the legal rights coming from the young man's bloodline and told the devil to go.

I then asked him what, if anything, he was experiencing. He very quickly told me that the devil had come out of him and was lying at his feet as a snake. Of course, this was all in the spirit realm. This young man, by the way, had no history in the church. He didn't understand prophecy or the ways of the Spirit of God. He was just having a spiritual encounter and knew that the demon that had controlled him was now at his feet. We then put underfoot the devil that had been required to come out of him. The legal right he was using to hold this young man was broken.

Jesus said in Luke 10:19 that serpents and scorpions and all the powers of the devil could not hurt us.

Behold, I give you the authority to trample on serpents and scorpions, and over all the power of the enemy, and nothing shall by any means hurt you.

Jesus was very clear that He had granted us all authority over the powers of the devil. We simply need to put him under our feet. Once the ancestral issues that the devil was using against this young man were revoked, he was free to be free. The people who had worked with him in the past commented on how they had never seen him hold his head up and his face shine as it did now after a very short time of ministry. The shame, guilt, and condemnation over his life had been broken. The main thing that allowed this was the very simple dealing with the legal rights of the devil from the bloodline. Once they were revoked, the power of Jesus' anointing set this young man free.

Why had the prayers before been ineffective in getting him free? Am I more *anointed* than the others who prayed for him? The answer is no. It wasn't about anointing. It was about having a legal right revoked that had allowed the devil to hold and torment this young man. If we are going to understand this, we must understand the Courts of Heaven and iniquity.

There is a very real *Court* in heaven. We see this in Daniel 7:10.

A fiery stream issued and came forth from before Him. A thousand thousands ministered to Him; ten thousand times ten thousand stood before Him. The court was seated, and the books were opened.

Daniel had an encounter in this Court. We can see in Daniel 7:25-27 that activity from this Court can cause great changes in the earth.

He shall speak pompous words against the Most High, shall persecute the saints of the Most High, and shall intend to change times and law. Then the saints shall be given into his hand for a time and times and half a time. But the court shall be seated, and they shall take away his dominion, to consume and destroy it forever. Then the kingdom and dominion, and the greatness of the kingdoms under the whole heaven, shall be given to the people, the saints of the Most High. His kingdom is an everlasting kingdom, and all dominions shall serve and obey Him.

What is being described here is what we would traditionally think of as the anti-Christ. We can at least say this is the anti-Christ spirit that works against the purposes of God in the earth. It declares the saints given into his hand for a period of time. This would mean they are *defeated.* Notice however that the *Court* is seated and renders a verdict from heaven. The result is the anti-Christ spirit's rights are revoked, dominion is taken away, and he is destroyed. The saints are then put back in charge and the kingdom and dominion are given to them. With one verdict from the Court of Heaven, the saints go from *defeat to dominion.* This is the power of operating in the Courts of Heaven.

When Jesus taught us on prayer in the Book of Luke, He placed prayer in three dimensions. He spoke of prayer as approaching God as Father, Friend, and Judge. In Luke 11:2, He showed God to be Father.

So He said to them, "When you pray, say: Our Father in heaven, hallowed be Your name. Your kingdom come. Your will be done on earth as it is in heaven."

God is our loving Father who loves to have us approach Him in faith and believe that He hears us. Jesus then placed prayer in approaching God as Friend. Luke 11:5-8 unveils this realm of prayer.

And He said to them, "Which of you shall have a friend, and go to him at midnight and say to him, 'Friend, lend me three loaves; for a friend of mine has come to me on his journey, and I have nothing to set before him'; and he will answer from within and say, 'Do not trouble me; the door is now shut, and my children are with me in bed; I cannot rise and give to you'? I say to you, though he will not rise and give to him because he is his friend, yet because of his persistence he will rise and give him as many as he needs."

Jesus continues His discourse on prayer by speaking of a friend approaching another friend on behalf of his other friend. The result is things being secured for a friend on his journey and one seeking to reach his destiny. Jesus was seeking to unveil that God wants to be our friend and how to approach Him in prayer in this manner. Jesus then reveals the third dimension of prayer in Luke 18:1-8—approaching God as Judge. He speaks of a widow who needs a verdict from an unrighteous judge.

Then He spoke a parable to them, that men always ought to pray and not lose heart, saying: "There was in a certain city a judge who did not fear God nor regard man. Now there was a widow in that city; and she came to him, saying, 'Get justice for me from my adversary.' And he would not for a while; but afterward he said within himself, 'Though I do not fear God nor regard man, yet because this widow troubles me I will avenge her, lest by her continual coming she weary me.'"

Then the Lord said, "Hear what the unjust judge said. And shall God not avenge His own elect who cry out day and night to Him, though He bears long with them? I tell you that He will avenge them speedily. Nevertheless, when the Son of Man comes, will He really find faith on the earth?"

The moral to this story is not that God is an unjust Judge. The moral is that if this widow who has no power to bribe an unjust judge can still get a verdict in her favor through a persistent presentation of her case, how much more can we see God our righteous Judge hear and move on our behalf! We, however, must know how to approach God as Judge in His legal, judicial system, which is the Courts of Heaven. To further understand this realm we must understand the word *adversary* in this story. *Adversary* is the Greek word *antidikos*. It means one who brings a lawsuit. This same word is found in First Peter 5:8.

Be sober, be vigilant; because your adversary the devil walks about like a roaring lion, seeking whom he may devour.

Notice that the adversary or *antidikos* in this verse is walking about. This means he is searching out that which he can use to build a case against us. His purpose is to build a case against us legally so he has the right to devour us. This is what is happening to so many people. The devil is devouring their lives, children, marriages, finances, health, destinies, and futures. They don't know why but they see it happening. They feel absolutely helpless to stop it.

The sources of this can often and frequently be found in the bloodline. The devil has discovered something in a person's bloodline that is legally allowing this to occur. The result is devastating things happening destroying lives and destinies. Through bloodline cleansing we can see any legal right of the devil to devour be revoked and removed. This is why Daniel and others would repent for their sins and the iniquities of their forefathers. They understood the iniquities of the ancestry were used legally by the devil to hold them in bondage and destruction. Daniel 9:16 shows clearly Daniel repenting for his sins and the iniquities of his forefathers. He then asked for mercy from the Lord.

O Lord, according to all Your righteousness, I pray, let Your anger and Your fury be turned away from Your city Jerusalem, Your holy mountain; because for our sins, and for the iniquities of our fathers, Jerusalem and Your people are a reproach to all those around us.

Daniel understood that their sins and the iniquities of the fathers before them had caused Israel to be in captivity and for

Jerusalem and Israel to be in reproach. If they were to come out of captivity and back into the blessing of God he needed to deal with what had caused it in the first place. This was their sins and the sins of the fathers. Isaiah 43:25-28 shows God speaking and telling the people to deal with the first father's sins so Israel can come out from under a curse.

I, even I, am He who blots out your transgressions for My own sake; and I will not remember your sins. Put Me in remembrance; let us contend together; state your case, that you may be acquitted. Your first father sinned, and your mediators have transgressed against Me. Therefore I will profane the princes of the sanctuary; I will give Jacob to the curse, and Israel to reproaches.

God is urging them to *state your case.* He then instructs them to deal with their *first father's sins.* Jacob (another name for Israel as a nation) was under a curse. Israel was under a reproach. A nation was losing its destiny because no one was coming before the Courts of Heaven and dealing with their sin and the sin of the fathers. This was essential to getting the captivity turned and God's people back under the blessing of God. The principle is we must deal not only with our sin that the devil would legally be using in the Courts of Heaven against us, but also the iniquity of our fathers. We must know how to come before the judicial realm of heaven and undo any case against us that Satan would bring. When we do, his rights to devour and destroy are revoked.

Iniquity of the fathers not dealt with can be used by the devil to destroy. Jesus even spoke of this. Matthew 23:29-32 shows Jesus chiding the religious leaders about their lack of repentance.

Woe to you, scribes and Pharisees, hypocrites! Because you build the tombs of the prophets and adorn the monuments of the righteous, and say, "If we had lived in the days of our fathers, we would not have been partakers with them in the blood of the prophets." Therefore you are witnesses against yourselves that you are sons of those who murdered the prophets. Fill up, then, the measure of your fathers' guilt.

Jesus said the same nature that was in the fathers was also in these. They would in fact do worse than their fathers. Their fathers killed the prophets and the righteous, but they would kill the very Son of God. Jesus tells them they will "fill up the measure of your fathers' guilt." In other words, what they will do as a result of the iniquity of the fathers fashioning their nature and desires will finish what is necessary. Even though Jesus must die for the sins of the world, it was the iniquity of the fathers producing the nature in these who would kill Jesus.

Iniquity fashions desires in us that are against the ways and purposes of God. This is why the devil can use the iniquities of our fathers as legal fodder to build cases against us. Jesus' heart was for these to repent. They, however, would not. If they would have repented and embraced Jesus as a nation, everything would have been different. God, however, in His foreknowledge knew they wouldn't. Jesus would then be killed by them because of the nature in them fashioned by the years of rebellion of their forefathers. I am citing this only to illustrate the power of iniquity not dealt with. If iniquity is not dealt with in the bloodline it can give the devil the legal right to use it against us and the purposes of God. We see this also in the promise God gave to Abraham in Genesis 15:13-16.

Then He said to Abram: "Know certainly that your descendants will be strangers in a land that is not theirs, and will serve them, and they will afflict them four hundred years. And also the nation whom they serve I will judge; afterward they shall come out with great possessions. Now as for you, you shall go to your fathers in peace; you shall be buried at a good old age. But in the fourth generation they shall return here, for the iniquity of the Amorites is not yet complete."

God promises Abraham that after his descendants are slaves in Egypt they will come out with great wealth and substance. He then tells him that there needs to be four more generations of iniquitous practices of the Amorites before God can righteously judge them and give the land to Abraham and his descendants. This tells us that iniquity in the bloodline is reason for judgment. The devil knows this. Therefore he comes and presents cases against people when there is iniquity in their bloodline. He on the basis of God's righteous standard presents cases requiring God to allow judgment against people. This is not the heart of God, but if the devil presents cases to require this, God as the righteous judge cannot disallow it. The only way this process can be stopped is through the blood of Jesus. The blood is the answer to the iniquity of bloodlines. We therefore have to know how to take the blood of Jesus and answer every request for judgment against us as a result of our bloodline. This is what Revelation 12:10-11 is speaking of.

Then I heard a loud voice saying in heaven, "Now salvation, and strength, and the kingdom of our God, and the power of His Christ have come, for the accuser of our brethren, who accused them before our God day and night, has been cast down. And they overcame him by the blood of the Lamb and by the word of their testimony, and they did not love their lives to the death.

The word *accuser* in the Greek is the word *katagoros.* It means a complainant at law. It is one who brings a complaint against you in a judicial system. It is speaking of the devil and his activity against us at God's throne or Court. Notice, however, that he is overcome by the blood of the Lamb. The blood of Jesus answers every accusation, case, and complaint against us. We must know how to take the blood of Jesus and silence any word speaking in contradiction to us. We can see every argument against us concerning our bloodline and the iniquity connected to it revoked and removed. When this is done the devil has just lost any legal right to resist, attack, or withstand the purposes of God. We are then free to move into all that we were created for. May every case against us be silenced and the passion and will of God be seen in our lives. The iniquity in our bloodline and any legal right of the devil to use it is revoked because of what the blood is speaking for us. Hebrews 12:24 tells us the blood is speaking for us.

To Jesus the Mediator of the new covenant, and to the blood of sprinkling that speaks better things than that of Abel.

The blood of Jesus is giving testimony on our behalf before the Courts of Heaven and the Throne of God. It is granting God the legal right to forgive and cleanse us and anything that would speak against us. We simply need to agree with the blood of sprinkling through confession and repentance. First John 1:9 tells us it is our confession that activates that which is for us.

If we confess our sins, He is faithful and just to forgive us our sins and to cleanse us from all unrighteousness.

When we confess and agree with what the blood is speaking in our behalf we are forgiven and cleansed. Through confession and repentance we embrace all that Jesus did for us on the cross. Everything that is speaking for us before His Throne becomes enacted for us. Not only is our own personal sin silenced from speaking against us, but the iniquity of the bloodline is silenced as well. We are now free because of what the blood is saying over our lives. Thank You so much, Jesus, for Your blood and sacrifice. The devil has no answer for the blood of sprinkling!

PART 2

PRAYERS FOR
APPLICATION

CHAPTER 9

REPENTANCE

Our son is ten years old and it is fun to see him grow and develop the personality God gave him. As parents we consider it our job to encourage and support him on his way. Part of it is sharing moral, social, and spiritual values.

One of those values is forgiveness and repentance. But sometimes it feels like hitting granite when an eight-year-old feels like he is right. I remember vividly how much resistance we got when we told him the first time that he had to apologize for his actions. Actually I must admit I was surprised to get so much opposition.

So he learned to ask for forgiveness. But it did not take him long to discover the positive effect of asking for forgiveness and its advantages. However, we then realized something else: He speedily developed the ability to ask for forgiveness by casually saying sorry without any remorse. His confession and readiness to ask for forgiveness were commendable; however, we now had to proceed to a more difficult part. We had to help him understand that an apology has to come from your heart and that you must be convicted about your wrongdoing.

The sacrifices of God are a broken spirit, a broken and contrite heart—these, O God, You will not despise (Psalms 51:17).

Repentance is not a method we can casually use and then continue as before. Repentance is a process and a decision to change and to pursue a different way. We confess that we have done wrong and are guilty; this is the way to receive forgiveness.

For you do not desire sacrifice, or else I would give it; You do not delight in burnt offering (Psalms 51:16).

David had a revelation about it that he wrote it down in Psalm 51. In verse 18, he declares that God does not care about methods; He just cares about receiving the right kind of offering. In verse 21, he says that God delights in the right kind of offering. An offering that includes the heart, which is pleasant before God and He cannot despise it.

There are many areas of repentance, but we would consider most of them as simple. We are aware of the fact that there are also experiences that are hard and oftentimes even painful. In these cases it is hard to repent sincerely and we understand that. This is why we have a wonderful helper—the Holy Spirit.

For I know that in me (that is, in my flesh) nothing good dwells; for to will is present with me, but how to perform what is good I do not find (Romans 7:18).

For it is God who works in you both to will and to do for His good pleasure (Philippians 2:13).

Even if everything on the inside of us resists repentance, we know that this is the right way to go, and we come to God asking Him to help us. And He is our helper. He is the one who works in us the will and the completion. And He is also the same who transforms us according to our repentance into a freedom we may not have had before.

THE BEGINNING

Psalm 100 says that we enter the courts of God with thanksgiving. Before we concentrate on these contracts and agreements, as well as on the iniquity and sin in order to repent from it, we want to start by worshiping God and giving Him glory so we come into alignment with Him. I have rephrased this a little bit to adapt it more to the way we express ourselves today.

Prayer

My father in heaven, I praise You with all of my heart and I lift up Your Name. No one is like You, Lord of lords and God above all gods. I delight in what You do. And one day, every nation will worship at Your throne, Lord. Everybody will glorify Your name, because You are great and You work miracles. You, O God, are God alone.

Today I ask You: Lead me more to live, think, and walk in Your ways. I want to live in complete alignment with You, without any compromise. I place my own ideas on Your altar and I want to open myself up for Your truth and clarity.

Where my heart and my thoughts wanted to elevate themselves against Your knowledge, I ask You: Give me the fear of the Lord that will help me to put Your truth, revelation, and knowledge above everything else.

I praise You, Lord, and I say that You are my God. With all of my heart I will praise Your name eternally. You are so eternally grateful to me. You have saved my soul from death and eternal condemnation and You want to help me to destroy covenants of sin and death. I rejoice and I am delighted.

I know that I can count on Your help and support. You help me to dispel everything so I can stand before You clean and holy and fulfill everything You have called me to before the foundation of the world.

Today I declare before the visible and invisible world, just as on the day of my salvation: You have given Your only Son, so that everyone who believes in Him shall be saved. Lord, I believe! I confess Jesus Christ, His cross, and His resurrection. There is no other God besides You. I believe in You and I stand in an eternal covenant with You.

With Your help I now want to consciously separate myself from everything that gives the enemy a right to hinder me because of my bloodline and I enter into the full potential and blessing.

PLACE YOURSELF UNDER THE PROTECTION OF GOD

When we break covenants that have given the enemy rights for thousands of years, he does not simply want to give up this territory without a fight. This is why we are entering a spiritual fight as we pray in this way. The enemy does not want to give up his territory freely and he would like to attack us in an unprotected area in our lives and circumstances. This is why it is important that we put ourselves—including everything that belongs to us, our families, relatives, friends, possessions, and everything that is in connection with us—under the protection of the blood of Jesus.

Advance Warning

It is possible that you decide to cleanse your bloodline and suddenly things pop up from different directions seemingly out of the blue. Suddenly you do not have time any more, no energy, or no possibility to take care of your bloodline. Or you feel tired, exhausted, weary, or you are overcome by distraction. Suddenly you feel unwell, you experience headaches, or other difficulties. Oh, and by the way—you better put that mobile phone far away so it won't distract you. All of these things are well-tried tricks of the enemy, trying to stop you getting into this area.

Prayer for Protection

Lord, with everything I have and I am, I want to ask for protection from You alone. I consciously place myself under Your protection so that the enemy cannot harm me in any way.

Because I make You a place of refuge in my heart, I become invulnerable just like being within a fortress. No matter what tries to attack me, You make sure that it cannot reach me.

I want to be so close to You, that You Yourself become my dwelling place. I want to be so strongly aligned that You are like a rock in times of storms for me.

Protection of the Family

Today and especially during this time of bloodline prayer, I put myself and my family under the protection of the blood of Jesus. In particular I put my children _____, _____ (say their names), including those yet to be born, under the protection of the blood of Jesus. I say: God is our fortress! The enemy is not allowed to touch us.

I put all our thoughts, feelings, relationships, and friendships under the protection of the blood of Jesus. I pray that angels will build an impenetrable wall around us. I bind every spirit of sickness, accident, strife, and misunderstanding. You have no right here. We stand under the protection of the blood of Jesus!

Protection of Relatives

Our experience has shown that relatives can become a particular target for the enemy during spiritual warfare—one of the reasons for that is probably because they are close to our hearts. That is why we pray particularly for those relatives who are not saved—that God will protect them from the powers of darkness, from being shaken up because of these prayers. As Christians it is our job to stand in the gap for those people who have not been saved yet. (We consciously call them those who are "not yet saved," so we would not put a yoke on them through our confession of calling them "unsaved.")

Father, I ask You for my relatives who are saved and for those who are not saved yet, that they will be put under the protection of the blood of Jesus. I pray that You would protect them, with Your great grace and love, where they cannot protect themselves.

Protection for Employees

I draw a bloodline around my workplace, my boss, and my colleagues. If you are looking for a job: *I put every job application, every job interview, and every possible initiation of an employment under the protection of the blood of Jesus.*

Protection for Entrepreneurs

I draw a bloodline around my business, my business partners, my co-workers, and my employees. I draw a bloodline around our accounts and everything that is connected to it (the tax advisor, accountant, laptops, tools, etc.).

I put all of our business plans and upcoming contracts under the blood of Jesus—all contractors and everyone who is in touch with me.

Finances, Property

I proclaim the blood of Jesus over my finances, my property, and everything that belongs to me—my car(s), my bank accounts, my debit and my credit cards, and every investment.

I proclaim the protection of the blood of Jesus on our homes, pets, and on everything that belongs to us.

The blood of Jesus is the greatest power of the universe. In the Name of Jesus every knee will bow, on the earth, in the earth, and under the earth. Every tongue must confess that Jesus Christ alone is Lord, and all bow to His rulership and authority (see Phil. 2:9-10).

No power, no force of darkness has the right and the possibility to gain access to our lives or anything that is connected to our lives.

CONFIRMATION AND RENEWAL OF MY DEDICATION

My Father, King, and Judge:

I want to live the days of my life in the way You have planned it and written it down in the book of my life. I want every rebellion, every selfishness, and every lust of the flesh that is standing in my way against Your will for my life to be removed. It is my desire that I will reach the desire and fulfillment for You alone, to live for Your Kingdom and righteousness alone.

Should something come to your mind where you give room to sin, rebellion, or false lust, take time now to repent of it. Turn from this wrong way.

According to Romans 12:1, by faith I now present to You my whole body, my whole being as a living and well pleasing sacrifice. I determine today to live in a way that is pleasing unto You, seeking Your Kingdom first and Your righteousness.

In the name of Jesus, I ask You to destroy every fortress of reasoning and every knowledge that elevates itself against God in my life, because You are my Savior.

Beloved Holy Spirit, I invite You into my heart. Please help me with the process of bloodline cleansing so that I will be transformed even more from glory to glory. It is my heart's desire that You would glorify Yourself through me, Jesus, through my life and my deeds.

Sometimes we overlook sin and wrong actions that we have. But they are not hidden to the spiritual world. This makes us invulnerable. That is why it is important that we pray for protection where we are not aware of any sin.

My God and my Judge, should there be sin in my life that I am not aware of, I now determine to dispel it from my life as soon as it comes to the light. Until then I ask You that You would cover and protect me with Your grace where I have lived unconsciously in sin and trespasses.

I ask You, Jesus, that these rights will be covered by Your blood and will not give the accuser any right to attack. Please help me to recognize where there are accusations against me in my bloodline. My decision is firm—I submit every area under the protection of the blood of Jesus and the Word of God.

I will bring to fulfillment what God promises in Colossians 2:14-15:

Having wiped out the handwriting of requirements that was against us, which was contrary to us. And He has taken it out of the way, having nailed it to the cross. Having disarmed principalities and powers, He made a public spectacle of them, triumphing over them in it.

I bring my life in total alignment with You and I say, "On earth as it is in heaven." This is the alignment for my life.

CHAPTER 10

TAKE OFF TOWARD FREEDOM

The way and decision you just took is not a playground; it can be compared to a spiritual surgery. You should be aware of this. It is a surgery at your deepest inner being. Deeper than any regular consciousness; you are not conscious of these covenants, but they are still connected to your life. So we are now talking about a Holy Spirit surgery on your heart, your soul, your bloodline, your entire life including your descendants. We have repeatedly seen that people feel weak or exhausted after bloodline prayer, just like after surgeries in real life.

Be prepared that you might need some extra sleep afterward and that you might not be at full capacity afterward, possibly also feeling awkward. Make room for some extra time and space to allow your soul and body to be restored by praise and worship in the presence of God.

Your soul, your spirit and your body may be in a time of transformation. Take this time and continue with these prayers; it is worth it!

CHRONOLOGY

The prayers in this book may be composed differently, yet they all include the following eight principles:

1. Confession

We confess before God the Judge that He is our God and that Jesus Christ is our Redeemer. Besides Him there is no other God.

2. Praise

Before the visible and invisible world we give God glory, honor, and praise.

3. Repentance

We ask for forgiveness for our personal lives, for our family, and for our ancestors all the way back to Adam.

4. Divorce, Separation

It is important that we separate from covenants that have been established with other gods and that still have an effect on our lives.

5. Asking for the Judgment of God

We ask that God would judge on our behalf, on the foundation of our confession, our proclamation, repentance, and divorce.

We therefore ask God as a Judge that we will be completely disconnected from those covenants.

6. Dissolving of Debt and Iniquity

A verdict in our favor may be tremendous, but we have to ask for the full elimination of debt and iniquity for all following generations.

7. Confession of Our Covenant with God

We confirm before the visible and invisible world that we only want to have one covenant. There is only one true God—the Father, the Son, and the Holy Spirit—there is no one else besides Him and we submit ourselves to Him.

8. Gratefulness and Shouts of Joy

We thank God the judge for His righteous judgment. We give him honor, shouts of praise, and worship.

These points are part of every bloodline prayer. They belong to the protocol that needs to be followed, but can vary in its chronology, because we want to pass the leadership to the Holy Spirit. The prayers in the following chapters may not appear systematically and identically structured in their procedure, but in their core they reflect the above given points.

By you deciding to pray your bloodline, you have made it clear to the enemy that you want to start the battle and win your rightful territory back. The enemy does not want to give it up without a fight, so he will make the way as difficult as possible for you. He will try to cause circumstances that will stop your triumphal procession.

And a great windstorm arose, and the waves beat into the boat, so that it was already filling. But he was in the stern, asleep on a pillow. And they awoke Him and said to Him, "Teacher, do you not care that we are perishing?" Then He arose and rebuked the wind, and said to the sea, "Peace, be still!" And the wind ceased and there was a great calm. But He said to them, "Why are you so fearful? How is it that you have no faith?" (Mark 4:37-40)

When Jesus took off with His disciples in a boat to the land of the Gadarenes, it was not a walk in the park for the disciples. In the middle of a sea they were surprised by a storm. It must have been so bad that the disciples feared for their lives, even though they were experienced fishermen. Jesus, utterly unimpressed and sleeping in peace, was woken up by them and then calmed the storm. But this was not a regular storm. I am certain that it was caused by spiritual powers in order to stop Jesus from His mission.

Jesus had a mission to accomplish there, which was to cast out a legion from the demonized Gadarene, who had held the whole area in fear and trembling. This legion did not want to simply give up their territory, so they tried to use natural circumstances to hinder Jesus' coming.

This is why we also place natural circumstances under divine protection and we ask God that the divine order surrounding us will be protected.

Prayer

Father in Heaven, thank You that You are not a God of disorder but a God of peace. Thank You that You do not waver in the midst of heavy storms but remain in peace. I ask You that You would protect my circumstances and my life in the order of Your Kingdom during this time of bloodline prayer and beyond.

Do not allow for any storms to come up that would hinder my breakthrough. No sicknesses, no relationship problems, no anger, frustration, and hopelessness. I bind any attack of the enemy on these times of prayer and cleansing and I command him to stay within his boundaries.

I am here and I open up to this cleansing to glorify You in my life. As Isaiah said, I also want to say: Lord, here I am, use me and send me.

As a next step, we take care of those four major covenants that I have written about in the previous chapters.

BLOOD COVENANTS

Blood covenants have a huge spectrum. They are established through the shedding of blood. It includes murder and suicide, sacrificing children as well as abortion, ritual offerings and animal offerings, mass murder and genocide; it includes the many wars with their massive bloodshed. There are more areas that may have been overlooked. One of them is the occult use of menstrual blood and the piercing of tattoos.

All of the above are things that are used to make covenant, and they need to be broken because they bring forth bondages and curses in our bloodlines.

Prayer to Dissolve Blood Covenants

Heavenly Father, I stand in Your presence to repent and to receive forgiveness. I am aware of the fact that I may not have been present in person but that I am guilty with my forefathers because I was in their loins and therefore participated in the execution of all these cruelties as well.

Heavenly Father, I repent for the shedding of blood that I am aware of because of my historical knowledge. I repent for the shedding of blood during the wars of the twentieth century. I repent for the shedding of blood during the first and second world war, during the Balkan war as well as all other wars that were caused by us Europeans and Westerners on all continents.

I ask for Your forgiveness that I have added to the establishment of such a huge blood altar in the twentieth century, the biggest blood altar humanity has ever seen. Forgive me, Father, and give me a heart of love, acceptance, and passion, even for my enemies.

My Father, I also repent for those wars that I do not know about, because they are too far back in my past—wars my ancestors were involved in and wars they have tolerated. I ask for Your forgiveness for every blood covenant all the way back to Adam. I repent for myself and my ancestors on my mother's and my father's side all the way back to Adam. I confess that I am guilty of every war that my ancestors were involved in and I ask for Your forgiveness.

I repent for abortions and sacrificing children to Moloch. Father, I ask for Your forgiveness for myself and my ancestors all the way back to Adam.

Father, for this iniquity and these false covenants I receive what Jesus paid for with His completed work at the cross. I cancel every contract we established consciously or unconsciously. I also do not want any profit that would be mine as a result of these covenants. I absolve myself from this treaty and all its rights and obligations and I receive the redemption and forgiveness for those trespasses by the blood of Jesus.

Father, I claim the blood and the completed work of Jesus. Righteous Judge, Your Word says that Jesus did not just come in water, but also in water and blood. I receive the redemption and forgiveness of the trespasses through the blood of Jesus according to Your riches in glory and Your grace. With the offering of Jesus I was sanctified; perfect this work in me, Lord, and make me complete.

In full consciousness and by faith I now leave all blood covenants of my forefathers all the way back to Adam, and I decide to enter into a blood covenant with Jesus.

My King, I ask You that my name and the name of my ancestors will be erased from these blood covenants and altars. I ask You that from this moment on all other accusations will be cleansed and judged on the basis of the blood covenant of Jesus.

SEED COVENANTS

According to the Bible, sexuality belongs inside the marriage covenant. If sexuality is practiced outside of marriage, covenants and curses are established that we need to be set free from. These include premarital intercourse, masturbation, intercourse with people of the same sex, rape, pedophile activity, sexually aroused touch of children including abuse, ritual and sexual abuse, intercourse with animals, pornography, sexual fantasies, and much more. One of the greatest achievements of the enemy may well be that he convinced people that he and his deeds do not truly exist.

A friend of mine who works as a pedagogue at a social service center told me that his designated area was a stronghold of ritual sexual abuse. He takes care of people in great numbers who share about the ritual sexual abuse they have gone through, executed by people in positions of power.

For many of us this is hard to imagine; it sounds like made-up stuff. But because we live in this rational, illuminated age, it does not mean that the spiritual world has been extinguished. The enemy has managed to convince people, especially in the West, that these things are simply crazy inventions so that he can easily advance his agenda. *As I said, the enemy's greatest victory may well be that he persuaded people of his non-existence.*

If you have been a Christian for a while you most likely have heard about witchcraft in Asia, Africa, or South America. As bad as some of those rituals may sound, do not be deceived—there is high-level witchcraft happening in the West. The enemy aims always at executing power over individuals, people groups, nations, and continents. He wants to take their power away from them to take over. The simple fact that the western world "rules" over all those other territories and exploits them for its own purposes should cause any sharpened spiritual sense to be alarmed.

Without going into this any deeper, we should be aware of the fact that witchcraft in Europe and the western world display a more serious occult involvement. Unlike in Africa, the people who initiate and execute those dealings and rituals are less frequently people who are in the visible public, but those who have taken positions of power. Those are people who perform witchcraft in the background, in hidden places. In those circles, often sexual rituals are being performed with abuse that leads to covenants. What usually happens during a sexual union, something that is practiced during those sessions as well, is the release of seed, and this seed is an important part of the seed covenant. The seed has the potential to reproduce descendants and the enemy would like to have dominion over our descendants. Any place where your ancestors have given their seed to these covenants, you and your destiny were sold out to the enemy. We therefore should make sure we dissolve these covenants.

Prayer

Heavenly Father, You have given the instruction to the Israelites to be circumcised on the eighth day as a sign of sanctification of their seed and descendants for Your glory.

Today I confess for myself and my ancestors on my mother's and father's side that we are guilty of not having dedicated our seed to You but rather to the lust of the flesh. We have sinned, and I ask You for forgiveness of my sin and the sins of my forefathers all the way back to Adam.

I repent for any prostitution, perversion, ritual sexual practices, sodomy, homosexuality, sexual covenants and altars, polygamy, adultery, incest, masturbation, and pedophilia.

Father, I confess these things on my own behalf and on behalf of my bloodline; I plead guilty, and I ask for Your forgiveness.

Father, these sins and trespasses go against my own body and against You and Your principles, Your Kingdom, and Your holiness. My King, I ask You to forgive me where I actively served at those altars and where I supported the expansion of the kingdom of darkness through it. Because those altars give the kingdom of darkness power and they are supposed to hinder the expansion of Your Kingdom.

I ask You that the blood of Jesus would wash away all guilt in my life and in my bloodline. I do not want to have anything to do with it.

Lord, wherever my name is written on those altars I ask You to erase my name from those altars, no matter where on earth or in heavenly regions they may be. Wherever my DNA may be connected to these altars, I ask You to release me through the precious blood of Jesus.

I ask for Your forgiveness for every trading platform on which I offered my seed and where I knowingly and through my own decision and will participated in that trade. Father, I confess that this trade is not a righteous trade, and this trade is a twist and is undermining Your love, grace, and mercy. Forgive this unrighteous trading of my seed and the seed of my forefathers all the way back to Adam.

I ask for Your forgiveness where my ancestors have entered trades, where our seed was consciously sold to the devil. Father, I confess that this trade is not a righteous trade; it undermines Your love, grace, and mercy. Forgive this unrighteous trade with my seed and the seed of my forefathers all the way back to Adam.

By faith I now claim Your forgiveness in the blood of Jesus. I receive my justification by Jesus Christ and His sacrifice.

Righteous Judge, I ask You to refuse admittance of any accusations of the accuser that he would bring fourth on the foundation of sexual covenants as well as seed covenants. I ask You on the basis of the righteousness and the sacrifice of my kinsman redeemer Jesus Christ that these accusations will be repelled and that the accuser will be rejected by the blood of Jesus and the testimony of His mouth.

I ask You with all of my heart: Make me a living sacrifice on Your altar, which is the sacrifice that is pleasing to You. Change me so that I and my life will become a well pleasing offering to You. So that I will bring honor, praise, and worship that will ascend to You as a well pleasing aroma. My God and my King, I vow to You and I proclaim before the visible and invisible world that my life, my seed, and my trading belong to the Father, the Son, and the Holy Spirit. My covenant is with Him and with Him alone. My life serves the glorification of Jesus Christ, His cross, and His resurrection.

I pray that all DNA in my blood and in my cells will come into alignment with the creational order of God. Come back to Your first estate that God had planned for You from before the foundation of the world.

Thank You, my Lord and my King, that You have cleansed me and that You have declared Your forgiveness toward me and that because of the blood of Jesus You judge on my behalf.

Thank You, Father, for the freedom that You have given me and allowed me to step into now.

WORD AND MEAL COVENANTS

A part of the meal covenant has already been covered alongside the blood covenants.

Word covenants can be things that have been spoken over you or that you may have confessed about yourself. Do not let us take these things lightly, because confessions have great power. It is truly amazing how almost every person can remember moments in their past when they were hurt or wounded by words. For example, I experience that people who were not even close to me or very well known said words that are still engraved into my memory, therefore in my feelings, and consequently my actions. Even lightly expressed foolish talk can have negative consequences for other people.

Unfortunately, our society has developed into a direction that giving our word does not have the weight that it used to have. Giving a handshake and a word have been replaced by many thorough contracts and documents set up by lawyers.

But the fact that in our Western world things have developed in such a way does not mean that it is the same in the spirit. Here are a few examples of how God sees it in His Word:

When you make a vow to God, do not delay to pay it; for He has no pleasure in fools. Pay what you have vowed—better not to vow than to vow and not pay.

Do not let your mouth cause your flesh to sin, nor say before the messenger of God that it was an error. Why should God be angry at your excuse and destroy the work of your hands? For in the multitude of dreams and many words there is also vanity. But fear God (Ecclesiastes 5:4-7).

But those things which proceed out of the mouth come from the heart, and they defile a man (Matthew 15:18).

But I say to you that for every idle word men may speak, they will give account of it in the day of judgment. For by your words you will be justified, and by your words you will be condemned (Matthew 12:36-37).

We see what kind of power our words, vows, and talk contain. And then of course there is this well-known Scripture from Proverbs 18:21: "Death and life are in the power of the tongue." This should be sufficient reason to repent for our own words and to repent for our ancestors.

Let us not use our words lightheartedly, but let us use them with power and influence that God has ascribed to them. We want to keep in our mind and hearts that Proverbs 12:18 says that the words of a chatterer are like the piercing of a sword but that the tongue of the wise promotes healing.

Prayer

Lord, I plead guilty for all the word and meal covenants with other gods that my ancestors and I have entered all the way back to Adam.

Father, I ask for Your forgiveness that we have used our words like swords hurting people. I ask for Your forgiveness where we put curses on our own lives and on the lives of others. You have given us a mouth to bless, forgive, and heal. But we have used it to give room to our anger, bitterness, and to our own lust.

Father, forgive us where we have received words and curses that have released negative things in our lives. I repent where I have been in agreement with them and where I thereby have entered into a word covenant.

Father, today I want to resolve those word covenants and I want to be in agreement with Your word covenants only. I detach myself from every wrong word and declaration, every curse, and every wrong word covenant of myself and my ancestors all the way back to Adam. I dismiss this covenant with You. I pray that the blood of Jesus will discharge me completely from these covenants and their effects.

I break the power of those word covenants over my life in Jesus' name.

I know that You, Lord, have thoughts of peace and welfare for me and that You only have covenants of well being for me. Your words give me hope and a good future.

Forgive me, Lord, where I and my ancestors have entered meal covenants that were not celebrated to honor You. Where we considered ourselves to be Christians yet we participated unworthily at the table of the Lord—I ask for Your forgiveness.

I repent for every meal covenant and every participation at the table of demons that we have participated at ceremonies of false gods. Father, forgive me where I ate raw meat and drank the blood of animals. Forgive me for participating in cannibalism and the exchange of arms with other gods and worshipers of false gods.

Father, I thank You for the power of the blood of Jesus Christ in my life. This blood destroys every word and meal covenant that held me and my descendants in captivity.

I pray that the DNA in my blood and in my cells will come into alignment with the Word of God. Come back into Your original estate that God has planned for you from before the foundation of the world.

I proclaim to the visible and invisible world that I have died with Christ through my baptism. Therefore, every evil word and meal covenant that has been established by me and my family all the way back to Adam is cancelled.

In Christ I have risen to newness of life. Through Christ I have become a new creation—old things have passed and new things have come. With the covenant through Christ I step into a new future of blessing and favor. I thank You, Lord, for the powerful blood of Jesus Christ.

SALT COVENANTS

As mentioned before, salt covenants pertain to three important areas of your life and faith. Colossians 2:17 reveals that the things of the Old Testament are shadows of things to come. They are revelations and pictures that concern us today and from which we can receive knowledge and understanding.

Which are those three areas that are affected by salt covenants? On the one hand it is your priesthood in Christ, because God has entered an eternal salt covenant with the priesthood.

Second, the salt covenant affects your kingship in Christ, because the salt covenant was cut with the house of David and his kingship.

And third, it applies to the ground and the land to which we have been called to bring them into the same state as in heaven.

Salt covenants are full of power. God has placed us on the earth as salt, so we are an expression of His salt covenant with this world. He wants to enter a covenant with our nations. In order for this to happen, we dissolve those salt covenants that do not honor and glorify God and cause us to become flavorless.

Prayer

Heavenly Father and righteous Judge, my final request now is the dissolving of the fourth of those major covenants that I know from Your Word.

I ask for Your forgiveness that I and my ancestors entered salt covenants that gave the enemy a right to negatively influence my priesthood, my kingship on the earth, and at the same time empower the kingdom of the enemy. I admit being guilty of having entered salt covenants on heights, regions, nations, and continents. I admit my guilt to have established a false priesthood and kingdom, which was not established as part of Your Kingdom, but it served my passions, my selfishness, and my flesh.

I declare before the visible and invisible world that I do not want to have anything to do with these covenants. I ask for the resolving of those covenants on the basis of my confession, my repentance, and my righteousness through the blood and the cross of Jesus.

My King, I ask for the cleansing of my bloodline from every evil salt covenant all the way back to Adam.

My Lord, I come to You through Jesus, who is the mediator of the new covenant and in whom the blood of sprinkling speaks better than the blood of Abel. In full awareness and out of my free will I have decided to step into the covenant of the blood of Jesus Christ, and I claim it for the rest of my life and the life of my descendants.

Work inside me according to Your will and transform me to be salt on the earth that is not flavorless but salt that You use to establish an eternal covenant on the earth.

I ask You, Lord, that all DNA in my blood and in my cells will come into alignment with the Word of God our Creator.

Come back into the first estate that God had planned for you from before the foundation of the earth.

Lord, use me to do Your will and to expand Your Kingdom so that it will be on earth as it is in heaven.

Righteous Judge, I thank You that You have removed every salt covenant and every resulting curse from me. I love You!

CHAPTER 11

TYPICAL FOR EUROPEANS

The title "Typical for Europeans" is very broad and can certainly be divided into multiple sections. But in this part of the bloodline prayer I want to talk about the guilt we need to be cleansed from because of things that were specifically done in the European and European-influenced region. We want to resolve covenants that we repeatedly encounter when specifically praying bloodline prayers.

The name of our continent shows who it has been dedicated to and to whom all people who are originally from Europe have been dedicated. A little later in this book I will quickly describe the marriage-like covenant with Europa.

We can always divide Europe into smaller areas and regions. Even parts of cities differ from each other and have their own history and character. But to enlarge on that is beyond the scope of this book.

Here is an example where the Bible confirms that certain areas reflect certain characteristics:

One of them, a prophet of their own, said, "Cretans are always liars, evil beasts, lazy gluttons." This testimony is true (Titus 1:12-13).

Obviously, Paul was aware of the fact that certain areas and nations have certain characteristics that are clearly visible for others. For instance, Germans are known for their punctuality, order, and precision, but not so much for humor and charm. Does that mean that there are no Germans who are unpunctual, disorderly, or who are humorous? Absolutely not! But those are statements concerning classical main characteristics that are particularly striking.

It is truly exciting to see what happens during bloodline prayer and how we continually can keep bumping into the same thing over and over again as we pray the bloodlines of people from similar areas. We can see that the culture of whole regions and nations is passed on as an inheritance, and that it happens much further than just to the third and fourth generation.

Enough said and explained. I think it is clear what I wanted to share. In our prayers, we now want to dedicate ourselves to those typically European matters.

EUROPE AND THE BULL

Originally Europa is a figure taken from Greek mythology. Europa was an attractive daughter of the Phoenician king Agenor and his wife Telephassa. Zeus transformed himself into a bull and took beautiful Europa on his back and brought her to Crete. There he had three sons with her. The name of the continent Europe is derived from this mythological figure.

This story is a mythological one and not a historical one, and that's the way we have to understand it. However, we should not leave out of our sight that these accounts can also be traced back to historical events, which with time have continually been amplified.

Now it came to pass, when men began to multiply on the face of the earth, and daughters were born to them, that the sons of God saw the daughters of men, that they were beautiful; and they took wives for themselves of all whom they chose. … There were giants on the earth in those days, and also afterward, when the sons of God came in to the daughters of men and they bore children to them. Those were the mighty men who were of old, men of renown (Genesis 6:1-2,4).

We can see here that spiritual beings that are called sons of God had fellowship with the daughters of men. It refers to fallen spiritual beings, because they sinned.

In the eyes of God, these activities came to such an excess that God had no other choice but to destroy the world that was known back then through the flood. It was the only way the only righteous and blameless seed on the earth, which was in Noah, could be protected and upheld.

From a historical and mythological point of view Zeus is one of many names for an idol called Baal. Baal is a Phoenician and Canaanite god that has many guises, the bull being the most common one.

The Hebrew word *baal* means lord, owner, husband, and king. We can immediately see the parallel to the true God of Christianity—the Lord, owner, and King, God Himself. Lucifer tries to take God's place through the god Baal, intending to delude man away from the right path.

It is time that our continent and the continents of the earth with their wrong covenants and lying gods will be dissolved and that we finally enter into the covenant with Jesus Christ. It is time that the things Jesus Christ has commissioned us to do will be seen—that entire nations will be baptized in the name of the Father, the Son, and the Holy Spirit.

Go therefore and make disciples of all the nations, baptizing them in the name of the Father and of the Son and of the Holy Spirit (Matthew 28:19).

It is time for a worldwide revival, reformation, and transformation. All of this starts with us and our personal divorce from Baal.

Prayer: Personal Confession of Guilt for Myself and My Ancestors

My beloved Father in heaven, I come before You and I repent for myself and my ancestors on my mother's and father's side all the way back to Adam, where we entered a covenant with Baal. I ask for Your forgiveness that we chose Baal as our lord, king, husband, and god. I plead guilty for the establishing of those covenants and for the fact that our lives and the lives of our descendants were given into his hands and possession.

Request to Divorce Baal

My Lord and King, by faith I step into the heavenly court and I ask You to divorce me, my life, and my descendants from Baal and all his rights. Lord, I ask that all claims of ownership from Baal on my life will from this moment on be denied. I do not want a covenant with Baal. I do not want to serve him. I ask for a divorce though the blood of Jesus. I ask You to put a dividing bloodline between me and every altar of this covenant with Baal.

Today I submit myself fully to Jesus Christ. I consciously decide to be in covenant with Jesus Christ alone until death and to serve Him for all eternity.

I testify here and now that Jesus Christ is my only Lord and Savior, who has paid a much higher price for me and my descendants. *He has purchased me with a high price and today and forever He is my Redeemer, Lord, Owner, King, Husband, and God. I have no other god besides Him; I do not want to serve any other god. I give myself and everything that belongs to me as His possession for all eternity.*

Affirmation of the God-Given Divorce

I thank You, God, for this divorce. I declare before the natural and spiritual world that I have been divorced from Baal as my king, lord, god, and husband. From now on neither I nor my descendants nor my possessions nor anything that is connected to me is in any covenant with Baal, because I am no longer subject to him; I do not owe him anything. We have been divorced.

Resolution of the Effects of Those Covenants

My King, my Lord, my God, and my Husband, on the basis of my repentance and my conscious divorce from Baal I ask You to redeem me from any effect of these covenants with Baal. I ask You to erase every claim of Baal on my life and declare it as illegal.

I used to be afar of but through Jesus I have been purchased with a high price and through the blood of Christ I have come close to God.

My righteous Judge, on the basis of Colossians 1:21-22 I plead that I will be taken out of every connection and every claim of Baal on my life. I plead that Baal and all of his claims will be brought to nothing forever. Father, I confess that I and my ancestors all the way back to Adam were once estranged from God, being His enemies in our minds and through our evil deeds. However, in the body of His flesh and participating in the death of Jesus I have become holy, justified, and without blame before You because I cling to You by faith and because I am determined to remain firm.

Declaration of the Newness of My Life

I confess before the visible and invisible world that I belong to You, Jesus Christ, and to You, Holy Spirit, and to You, my God and Father. I have decided to give You myself everything that belongs to me and everything I will ever have without holding anything back. My covenant is with You and with You alone. You are and remain in all eternity my King, my God, my Lord, and my Husband. I want to belong to You alone, now and forevermore. Amen.

EUROPEAN GODS

Before the development toward the so-called Christian western world, Europe went through many different phases of ruling structures. Most people are aware of the Roman Empire, possibly antique Greece and its expansion, or maybe the Celts.

However, most do not know much more about their historical background.

Actually, Europe was saturated by gods and idolatry. If we start in the south there are the Roman, Greek, Slavonic, Illyrian, Lusitanian, Etruscan, and Hungarian gods. Further north of course there was Germanic, Baltic, Samian, and Finnish idolatry with all its structures and forms. In addition to that we have all the influences of other areas such as antique Egypt, Babylon, and in present-day history the influence of Islam. Of course Islam does not belong to Europe, but we cannot deny its influence, as European nations such as Albania, Kosovo, parts of Bosnia, and Herzegovina consist of a Muslim majority.

Just as it was necessary in regard to our covenants with Baal, we first have to divorce ourselves from all paganism, including its assorted characteristics and presentations, before we then dissolve our bloodline from it.

The following gods and the idolatry connected to them have the same root and source. Often they are the same god who, under a different name, appears in different cultures. From our experience we know that these gods make their own claims, but of course they serve the kingdom of darkness. This is why a majority of gods have to be called by their names so we can specifically divorce them.

This list could be very extensive, and I want to avoid that. However, should you notice while praying that the Holy Spirit points out certain gods to you, take the following list and redeem your bloodline from it.

So let us proceed to prayer and get our divorce papers. The dynamic of this prayer differs from the other ones. On our biblical foundation we stand on the following Scripture while praying:

Therefore we also, since we are surrounded by so great a cloud of witnesses, let us lay aside every weight, and the sin which so easily ensnares us, and let us run with endurance the race that is set before us (Hebrews 12:1).

But you have come to Mount Zion and to the city of the living God, the heavenly Jerusalem, to an innumerable company of angels to the general assembly and church of the firstborn who are registered in heaven, to God the Judge of all, to the spirits of just men made perfect, to Jesus the Mediator of the new covenant, and to the blood of sprinkling that speaks better things than that of Abel (Hebrews 12:22-24).

Prayer

My Father, in Your presence and in the presence of the church of the firstborn, the spirits of the righteous men made just, the Holy Spirit, and Jesus Christ the Redeemer of the new covenant, I have decided to be divorced from all gods and idols to become His possession alone.

Father, I ask You for forgiveness for myself and my entire family line, for every covenant that we entered with other gods where we worshiped them, glorified them, and brought offerings to them. I recognize my iniquity and the trespasses of my forefathers all the way back to Adam. I repent for this unfaithfulness and today I ask You to execute and confirm my divorce from those idols.

My King, I divorce myself from all idols and figures resembling gods, from giants, and from all covenants belonging to them including their effects on my life and the life of my descendants.

My Father, I plead guilty for myself and my family for those covenants and today I want to be divorced from them.

I divorce any covenant with Zeus, Poseidon, Hestia, Hermes, Hera, Hephaestus, Hades, Dionysus, Demeter, Athena, Artemis, Ares, Apollo, Aphrodite, Allah, Coeus, Crius, Cronus, Hyperion, Iapetus, Mnemosyne, Oceanus, Phoebe, Rhea, Tethys, Theia, Themis, Eros, Jupiter, Neptune, Juno, Mars, Venus, Bellona, Janus, Vesta, Quirinus, Vulcan, Volturnus, Portunus, Pomona, Palatua, Furrina, Flora, Falacer, Ceres, Carmentis, Baldur, Bragi, Dellingr, Forseti, Freyr, Heimdallr, Hermod, Hoder, Loki, Mani, Mimir,

Meili, Odin, Thor, Tyr, Vili, Baduhenna, Bil, Beyla, Eir, Freya, Frigg, Fulla, Nanna, Sol, Syn, Jofur, Astrild, Balder, Ostara, Nerpuz, Frija, Gausus, Hretha, Mane, Sigel, Donar, Ziu, Wotan, Cernunnos, Airmed, Belenus, Borvo, Brighid, Grannus, Lugh, Belenos, Sulis, Damona, Swquana, Epona, Macha, Matronae, Lugh, Taranis, Toutatis, Esus, Sucellus, Ogmios, Tarvos, Trigaranus, Victoria, Bacchus, Mercury, Hercules, Maia, Hygieia, Minerva, Dazbog, Jarilo, Lada, Vesna, Morana, Perun, Rod, Svarog, Svetovid, Triglav, Veles, Zaria, Ziva, Zorja, Belobog, Berstuk, Dodola, Flins, Hors, Ipabog, Myesyats, Zimitra, Peklenc, and all other gods that have made claims upon me and my family.

My Lord, I claim that all gods and demons have to bring their claims and accusations to make them public, so that I and my bloodline can be redeemed from them by the testimony of my mouth and the blood of Jesus.

Father, I also ask You that all claims and accusations that are being brought forth from other gods will be claimed now or that they will remain silent forever.

My King, I ask You to confirm this divorce and the redemption of my bloodline through the blood of Jesus Christ as well as this new covenant I stepped into.

Seal my redemption form all Roman, Greek, Slavonic, Illyrian, Lusitanian, Etruscan, Hungarian, Samian,

Finnish, German, Arab, Egyptian, Babylonian, and Islamic idols. I ask You and I pray that every effect of these gods on my life and the life of my bloodline will henceforth be considered illegal and declared as such.

Father, I ask You that You would release me from any perverted cosmic influence from the stars, the planets, the natural and the supernatural world. Release me from the weather and its influence on me. Release me from the moon and its influence on my sleep and rhythm of life. Redeem me from false covenants with the earth and their influence on my health.

Father, I ask You to redeem me through the blood of Jesus Christ from every area of influence of the enemy and god who had legal rights in my life due to those old covenants.

My Lord, I come in agreement with Your Word and I say that my citizenship is in heaven and I am a citizen of heaven. I have placed myself completely under Your government, power, and authority.

I confess that it is no longer I that live, but Christ who lives in me. I declare that the accusation of those idols, who are not God, have to be more powerful than the grace of the blood and cross of Jesus Christ to surround me and my bloodline. But in faith and firm affirmation I confess—those gods do not exist.

Father, I thank You for Your grace, goodness, mercy, and redemption! I thank You that You have put all gods into their boundaries and that You bound them up with iron chains. Amen!

ALTARS

In Europe there are many quite well-known and some not-so-known altars from the past centuries and millennia. Examples of well-known altars are Stonehenge in the south of England, the Zeus temple of Olympia in Greece, the Amphitheater in Rome, the Pergamum Altar in Berlin, and countless churches that used to be temples for other gods that today are known as church buildings. The Pantheon in Rome, for instance, is a heathen temple that has been rededicated as a church building and today it is called the Santa Maria ad Martyres church.

When we talk about temples and altars, we usually think about their architecture or whatever was established in that place and about the occult practices that have taken place there. Yet this is only a small part of the purpose of those buildings. Historically these places have influenced, formed, and led entire societies. Trade has taken place in those places and therefore the economy of that region was empowered from there. Teaching, revelation, knowledge, moral values, laws, and protocols came forth out of these places.

There is a great connection between the welfare or economy of the region and the altars and the temple, so people were very zealous to keep that system in place. This becomes particularly clear in the rise of Demetrius in Acts 19, when the Gospel message endangered their economic system to go bankrupt.

Over years and centuries these systems were kept alive; simply their form and appearance changed. Our banking system feeds from the same source of these systems.

The church has renamed a great part of the idols of other religions. They gave them new names so that they could continue to worship them. Temple buildings were simply remodeled into church buildings, but the ceremonies basically do not differ much from the original occultism. This list could be extended on and on, but we are not here to list those practices but to point out the need to get a divorce from these things.

Prayer

Father, I repent for myself, my family, and my ancestors all the way back to Adam where we brought offerings at the altars and temples of Europa. I ask for Your forgiveness for any place where we looked for financial success in those temples and where our economy was sustained by it. Lord, I ask for Your forgiveness and I confess being guilty to having received and accepted this teaching, the orders of these idol altars and temples, and where we made them our own. Please forgive us where we received, tolerated, and practiced the teaching of the Nicolaitans. I ask for Your forgiveness that my ancestors received those teachings for the sake of their economic or social success. Father, I repent for all these attitudes and actions and I ask You to forgive us.

I repent for every offering that we have brought at the altar in the temple of Europa. Lord, I ask You to erase my name from the altars of Stonehenge, the Zeus temple, the altar of Pergamum, and from all temples and altars whether they are known today or not. I plead guilty to having mixed Your truth and laws with idolatry. I ask for Your forgiveness for where my ancestors and myself have not separated ourselves from this blasphemy but simply added faith to the existing paganism and idolatry.

Please forgive me for any participation and partaking at the altars and temples of Europa.

I confess today and for all eternity: You are the only God who has created the heavens and the earth. My King, You are the God who existed from all eternity and who will remain forever. There is no one else like You who is worthy of our worship, adoration, and honor.

Father, I am a part of Your church and ekklesia that Jesus Christ redeemed for Himself by His blood. I divorce every fellowship and partaking in the temples of Europa and I proclaim that I have decided to be in fellowship with the saints. This is why I walk in the light, like You are in the light, and the blood of Jesus, Your Son, cleanses me from every sin.

My King, I receive the purification and sanctification through the blood of Jesus and I ask You to detach me from all those temples and altars and cause me to become a clean, holy, and pleasing temple of the Holy Spirit.

FREEMASONRY

A lot has been discussed, speculated, and written in regard to freemasonry in the last years in Christian circles. I do not want to add anything to it, but I want to go straight to the prayer of repentance from it. We all certainly have to resolve our covenants with freemasonry.

Prayer

Father, I repent for the participation in networks that wanted to claim world government instead of acknowledging the earth as Your property. I ask for Your forgiveness for my natural and spiritual participation in freemasonry and all humanistic ideas that are revolting to You. My Lord, I repent for where my forefathers all the way back to Adam trusted in man-made systems inspired by the methods and systems of darkness instead of believing You and laying our lives down for You.

I confess guilt to having denied charity and exploited other people in order to lead a comfortable, debauched life at their cost. Father, I ask for the resolving of these contracts and covenants of freemasonry. I repent for the exploitation of people and the third world and for their enslavement so I can get luxury goods. Forgive me where I exchanged my life for a life of debauchery instead of a life for the spreading of the Gospel. I plead guilty for having accepted covenants and contracts of freemasonry that promised success, status, safety, and riches to me. I repent for this selfishness and for the greed of my ancestors.

Lord, I ask for Your forgiveness and the resolving of any contracts and covenants with any freemasonry lodge.

As I step now on the sea of glass, I accept the trade of the blood of Jesus to take my life for Himself. *Please release me from the "gambling table" of freemasonry and the Illuminati and place me on the foundation of the cross of Jesus Christ into the Kingdom of His light and His love.*

I renounce every contract and covenant, promises and networks of freemasonry, including all privileges as well as every inheritance connected to it in the Name of Jesus. I decide to receive the inheritance of Jesus Christ and whatever may be connected to it.

Father, I claim the blood and sacrifice of Jesus Christ and I ask You that every inheritance and every connection to freemasonry will be cancelled from my life. My Lord, I claim to be judged according to First Peter 2:24 and to be released from any form of freemasonry. Through the confession of my sin I have completely accepted the sacrifice of Jesus Christ. He has taken my sins to the cross so that I would die to my sins here and now and live unto righteousness.

My Lord and King, I thank You for Your righteous judgment, my divorce from freemasonry, and for the rejection of every accusation of my accusers in regard to freemasonry.

CHAPTER 12

DIFFERENT REGIONS

We do many bloodline prayers and during these sessions we enter the courts of heaven on a regular basis. Unfortunately we are not able to take care of every request that is coming in because there are simply too many. Sometimes people have to wait for weeks and months for an appointment. This has caused us to write this book and to regularly offer seminars with deliverance as well as having workshops to train other believers in how to practically get activated in the courts of heaven.

We know that not every person has the same personality traits and ways of thinking, but these differ from region to region. These regionally different ways of thinking do not derive from the Kingdom of God but from the territorial powers over the area. We want to separate ourselves from them because our citizenship is in heaven and not on the earth. We want to prioritize reflecting heaven in our lives, and our culture has to be submitted to that.

We have listed areas from which we want to resolve our bloodlines. By praying for people from different regions, these keep popping up in the courts on a regular basis.

PRAYER TO CONFIRM MY CITIZENSHIP IN HEAVEN

My Lord and King, I confess before the visible and invisible world that I am not first of all a citizen of my nation. My citizenship is in heaven from where I expect the Lord Jesus as a Savior. He will transform our body of humiliation and bloodline that it may be conformed to the body of Jesus' glory according to the working by which He is even able to subdue all things to Himself.

Father, I want to be judged and released according to Your justice and righteousness on the foundation of my heavenly citizenship and the inheritance that is mine as a result of it and to which the blood of Jesus enables me.

REPENTANCE FOR CHARACTER TRAITS THAT OPPOSE THE KINGDOM OF GOD

I repent of every attitude and character trait that I and my family have allowed, cultivated, and passed on for centuries. I repent for abuse, pride, humanism, racism, rebellion, and perfectionism. I ask for Your forgiveness where these things have harmed the expansion of the Kingdom and where we have rejected, disrespected, and expelled numberless people— including ourselves.

I ask for Your forgiveness for bitterness, hatred, rage, and anger and where I justified it, even though I knew that those are not holy characteristics. Father, forgive me where I allowed this hatred toward my family, my friends, and also toward my enemies and opponents. I plead guilty for having judged people who were not in agreement with me. People from other cultural circles, different religions, nations, and convictions, as well as different social statuses.

Father, on the basis of my confession I ask You to make me to be conformed to Jesus, who acted with love, grace, and acceptance without having received anything beforehand. Father, make me like Jesus and reject the accusations of the enemy on the basis of me pleading guilty and the redemption of the sacrifice of Jesus.

RELIGION

Father, I ask for Your forgiveness for the dead fruit that my faith and the faith of my family have brought forth. I repent for where I placed higher significance on a denomination or a tradition than to the Word of God, the Bible, and the living faith of Jesus Christ or the guidance of the Holy Spirit and the river of the fresh water of the Spirit.

Father, I ask for Your forgiveness wherever I placed greater significance on denominations and their shape than on Your truths. I separate myself from unbiblical teachings and structures of Catholicism and Protestantism. I also separate myself from false teachings and structures of Lutherans,

Orthodoxy, Anglicans, and every other denomination— Baptists, Adventists, Pentecostals, Charismatics, Quakers, Methodists, Mennonites, Pietists, and every other Christian or non-Christian denomination.

Father, help me to see the greatness of Your Kingdom and to not be limited by man-made institutions. I am part of the victorious ekklesia here on earth and I do not want to get stuck in belief or thought patterns of any denomination.

COVENANTS THROUGH FORNICATION WITH ANIMALS AND DEMONS

Father, I confess my sin and the sin of my ancestors all the way back to Adam for every form of covenants with demons and vampires. We are guilty of all kinds of perversion and detestable things and practices with animals, demons, spiritual beings, and vampires. I ask for Your forgiveness for all atrocities and evil practices in our families. I ask for Your forgiveness for my mother's and father's bloodline all the way back to Adam. My Lord, there is nothing that justifies these impurities, but I am so glad that there is one person, Jesus Christ, who has the power and authority to deliver me from these covenants through His blood and to cleanse my past.

Father, I claim the sacrifice of Jesus and I ask for the cleansing of my bloodline from every form of perversion, fornication with animals, demons, spiritual beings, and vampires. I separate myself and my inheritance from every advantage that I and my family had received by following these practices.

Father, I ask You for me and my ancestors all the way back to Adam for forgiveness for every covenant that we have made by executing perversion with animals and by entering covenants with demonic beings.

Father, I desire the intimacy with the Holy Spirit and the fellowship of Jesus Christ as well as Your love, the love of my Father in Heaven.

For these sins, guilt and trespasses, resistance and covenants I confess guilty and I receive Your cleansing, forgiveness, and the redemption of the blood and cross of Jesus Christ.

In the Name of Jesus, I proclaim that these things no longer have any power over me and my life, and that they have been tread under the feet of Jesus forever.

GAMBLING, TRADE WITH TYRUS, MAMMON, SHEBNA, AND LUCIFER

When Jesus said that we cannot serve God and Mammon, he made clear, how powerfully finances pull at our hearts. If we want to follow God wholeheartedly but our heart also reverts to methods that are not pleasing to God, we position ourselves on wrong trading platforms. We serve at altars at which we should not serve as followers of Jesus.

God teaches us in His Word that we should not put our heart to quick money schemes. But sometimes we allow ourselves to be seduced instead of aligning our financial way with God by wanting to access riches and prosperity by gambling. Many times this is accompanied by pious sounding thoughts such as the idea of wanting to use this money for the Kingdom of God.

That way you erase the fact that we turn away from faith in God's provision and put our hope in chance and luck. Whether we may be doing this consciously or unconsciously, we are now trading on altars of Tyrus and Mammon. We have to separate ourselves and our bloodline from them so that the consequences of this guilt will not stand in the way of our blessings.

Lord, I repent for gambling, unrighteous trading and gain, as well as the desire to gain riches quickly. I ask for Your forgiveness for my readiness to lose money because I saw a small chance of the possibly becoming rich through it. But I was not ready to fulfill my calling, which God has laid out for me to gain wealth.

I ask for Your forgiveness for trading on false altars and gates. I repent for the trade with Tyrus, Mammon, Shebna, and lucifer and everyone else belonging to this circle. I repent for the unrighteous trade on fiery stones in the heavens and also on platforms in economy and gambling.

Father, I ask for Your forgiveness that I trusted more in the economy and the banking system, loan sharks, shares and bonds, and other kinds of investments than Your provision. I repent for my desire for riches and fast gained wealth. I ask You for myself and my family for repentance, Lord. Lord, forgive me my greed and that I held back that money from You to heap up riches for myself. I ask for Your forgiveness for where money, work, and success were placed before God and the building of His Kingdom.

My King, teach me to walk in Your righteousness in everything You give to me and to administrate according to Your will and Kingdom.

I separate myself from the trading platforms with Tyrus, Mammon, Shebna, and lucifer and I separate myself from all those trades.

My Lord, help me to be a righteous steward to whom You can entrust a lot, even authority over cities. Give me a heart that seeks Your Kingdom first. I want to believe that You will thus add everything else to me.

Lord, I resolve and separate myself from all these claims and I place myself into the rights of Your Kingdom, Your provision and multiplication on every level of my life.

MOON, WOLVES, AND LEVIATHAN

It would go beyond the scope of this book to specifically expand on these covenants that men have made with the moon, moon gods, and moon goddesses. Nevertheless, our experience showed us that separating from these covenants can resolve sleeping disorders, once the bloodline has come into new alignment with Christ in this area.

We offer you a general prayer to divorce this kind of idolatry. Some people had to specifically divorce from some idols in order to receive their breakthrough. It is easy to get a list of the different moon gods; one of them can simply be found on Wikipedia.

I ask for Your forgiveness for worshiping the moon and moon phases. Forgive me for every covenant with moons and moon gods. I ask Your forgiveness for where we made decisions based on star constellations instead of the Holy Spirit.

I divorce myself from the following moon gods: I divorce the North-Germanic moon god Mani, the moon god Thrud, the moon god Heimdall as well as Artemis, Callisto, Selene, Luna and Diana, Illat, Aliat, the Chinese moon god Chang'e and the Indian moon god Chandra, the moon god Ixchel of the Maya people, the moon god Tawac and the moon goddess Lakota of the First Nations people. Please forgive me where I have served these idols in any way or form. I separate myself from idolatry and ask You to erase my name and the names of my ancestors from these altars. I do not want any profit from these covenants. You alone are my God; I want to bring my life into full alignment with You and make my decisions by Your guidance alone.

I repent for every covenant and contract with the spirit of leviathan and the python spirit, as well as any earthly and heavenly beings of darkness.

Father, I deny worshiping them, I refuse each one of those covenants and contracts as well as every inheritance from them, and I declare that You, God, are the only one who is worthy to receive praise and adoration. I worship You alone in my life.

POLITICAL IDEALISM

Father, I ask for Your forgiveness for myself and my ancestors all the way back to Adam for the partaking in any political idealism that did not reflect Your Kingdom, Your righteousness, and Your justice. I repent for tribalism, socialism, communism, capitalism, liberalism, anarchism, feminism, atheism, humanism, genderism, environmentalism, Islam, and any other ideology that does not reflect Your Kingdom. Father, I renounce every political, social, and economic idealism and every structure and form of government that does not give glory to Your Kingdom. Lord, forgive me and my family where we have been more actively involved in those ideologies than in the spreading of Your Kingdom. Please forgive us where we thought that these ideologies were more important for the world than spreading Your Kingdom.

I ask for Your forgiveness for where we persecuted, disdained, and fought against these ideologies and their representatives instead of concentrating primarily on spreading Your Kingdom.

Father, I confess here and today (say the place, day, and time) *before the visible and invisible world and particularly before You as a righteous Judge that my citizenship is first and foremost in heaven and that I support the ideals, laws, and orders of Your Kingdom thoroughly. Father, on the grounds of the sacrifice of Jesus I plead that my bloodline and I will be separated from every idealism that does not serve the expansion of Your Kingdom, Your orders, Your ideals and moral values.*

I thank You, Father, that on the foundation of my repentance and Your absolution and the blood of Jesus I have been set free. And he whom the Son sets free is free indeed. And every principality, power, and accuser has to recognize this for all eternity.

MOTHER EARTH AND QUEEN OF HEAVEN

Lord, I repent for the contracts and covenants and connections to the so-called Mother Earth and the Queen of Heaven, to witchcraft, and to the occult. I confess my iniquity and the iniquity of my families all the way back to Adam. I confess that we made covenants and treaties with Mother Earth and the Queen of Heaven. Father, I ask You for forgiveness for every offering that we have brought, including baking cookies and cakes for the feasts of Jezebel and bringing animal or human sacrifices.

I ask for Your forgiveness, my King, that we placed curses on our entire bloodline and thus harmed Your Kingdom and the earth. Father, I separate myself today from Mother Earth and the Queen of Heaven. My Father, I ask that You would send Your fire on these altars, covenants, and contracts and completely erase my name, my bloodline, and my DNA from them so that no trace or remnant nor even the memory of it will be found in my bloodline any more.

I proclaim that my name, my bloodline, and my DNA through the blood and offering of Jesus Christ has been completely removed from these altars, covenants, and contracts, and that the accuser has no more rights to use them against me in court, in Jesus' mighty name.

BREAKING THE TEN COMMANDMENTS

My King, I ask for Your forgiveness for the breaking of Your laws and the laws of Christ. Father, forgive us where we have worshiped You and also other gods at the same time and where we prostrated ourselves before them and served them.

I repent for fabricating and producing pictures of idols. Lord, I repent for where my family has spoken Your name in vain and even cursed it.

I ask You for forgiveness for where we did not honor the day of the Lord and thus mistrusted Your provision.

Father, I ask Your forgiveness for not having respected my parents and where I considered them a burden rather than a blessing. I repent for every aversion against my parents because they may have been bad parents, because they left me or they did not take good care of me. No matter what they were like in the past or what they may be like, I want to forgive them now and I want to ask for Your forgiveness for my trespass of not honoring and respecting them.

I repent for every murder that has taken place in my family and I forgive every murderer who has taken lives in my bloodline.

I ask You for forgiveness for everything that has been stolen in my family where we have been selfish thieves rather than benefactors. Also I forgive any person who has stolen from me and my bloodline; I do not want restitution from them, but I trust that I will get restitution from You, my Father. Father, I pray that the sin of these people will be forgiven. I release them from their debt just as I have been released by the blood of Jesus.

My Lord, I ask Your forgiveness for desiring the wife of my neighbor. I repent for where I have looked at people lusting and where I have committed adultery with them in my heart or where I even acted it out. I ask for Your forgiveness for myself and my family and I ask You to give me a clean conscience and clean thoughts. Holy Spirit, help me to keep this holiness alive, which I have received now.

Father, forgive me of any jealousy and desire for the possessions of other people. I confess my guilt and the guilt of my forefathers—that we have begrudged them for their blessings.

CHAPTER 13

CLOSURE

If you have made it all that way to this part of the book, you have taken a huge step toward freedom and authority. Congratulations!

As a next step, I recommend you study the books *Navigating in the Courts of Heaven* as well as *Releasing Destinies from the Courts of Heaven* by our friend Robert Henderson. We believe that Robert has a great gift of explaining those truths.

Before we enter into courts of heaven, we have to prepare our case, which is one part of what we have done in the second part of this book.

Therefore if you bring your gift to the altar, and there remember that your brother has something against you, leave your gift there before the altar, and go your way. First be reconciled to your brother, and then come and offer your gift. Agree with your adversary quickly, while you are on the way with him, lest your adversary deliver you to the judge, the judge hand you over to the officer, and you be thrown into prison (Matthew 5:23-25).

These words of Jesus are very astounding because they are in contradiction to the conviction of many Christians. Jesus says that when we bring an offering and we remember that a brother has something against us that we should leave our offering at the altar and come to our brother quickly to reconcile with him.

Have a close look at this. The Word of God says that we have the responsibility to become active when our brother has something against us. Note that it does not say when we have something against him in our hearts. When he has a problem with us in his heart, we have to take the first step to bring reconciliation. Even for many Christians this is a serious challenge.

Why then is it so important that we have the proper attitude in our hearts? Verse 25 says that we have to approach our opponent quickly. Who is our opponent? It is important to understand that it is not our brother. It is a third party in this story. It is the accuser who wants to accuse us before God in his court. It is the one who would like to deliver us to the judge.

Have a look at what it means when a brother has something against us. We have to make an effort and to reconcile, because otherwise the accuser will find something to legally accuse us. But it goes even further. The word says that we will be given over to the servant who will then throw us into prison, and we will only leave this prison when the last penny has been paid.

What is a prison? It is a limitation of your liberty, your will, your authority, and your life. This is the goal of the accuser—he wants to emaciate and limit you. By redeeming our bloodline, we answer our adversary quickly so he cannot bring forth any righteous claims before the judge.

You may be telling yourself that many things are unfair. Actually, it is unimportant how we personally see and judge things. What matters is that our way of thinking and our will is in alignment with the will and Kingdom of God and the mind of Christ.

At this conclusion take the time to pray and ask the Holy Spirit whether there are people who have anything against you. In case you are aware of one person or several people the Holy Spirit reminds you of, then take the first step toward reconciliation. In case this person does not want to reconcile, you are released.

Reconciliation cannot be effectuated at any price. Sometimes people expect you to give up your faith in Christ, your family, or your calling before they will reconcile with you. Without question this is not possible and this is not what Matthews 5:23-25 is talking about. This is the reason why it says "your brother," which implies that you have the same basis of faith and belonging. If you pursue Christ, you will not be able to please everybody. But it is of highest priority to live in peace with the brothers and sisters of the same faith.

We have detached ourselves from many things and taken away legal rights from the adversary. Of course Jesus has done it all, but our repentance and proclamation have activated all of it.

In the introduction I mentioned that in regard to the things for which we have repented in the second part of this book it may simply be a certain foundation for a successful start in the courts of heaven. It is a start for your successful time in the courts of heavens. There will be many more accusations that the enemy will bring forth against you, and you will have to overcome them in the same way—through repentance, which is part of the testimony of your mouth, the blood of Jesus, and not loving your life until death.

THE DEVIL IS A LIAR

This is a statement we often hear when we speak about the devil. This statement is 100 percent right, because he definitely is a liar, and he has come to steal, kill, and destroy. Yet all of these things are illegal.

In case the enemy is guilty of any single one of these things in our lives, we have to turn around and summon him to court. So now we bring him before court. In this case it is a simple thing because God the righteous Judge will make a short process and judge on our behalf on the basis of His righteousness and justice.

Many times people suffer from unrighteous terror from the enemy, but they never bring it before the Judge of heaven and earth and simply endure it or they try to chase it away by many different means. The solution is that we bring him before court and that we will allow our heavenly Father to judge him just like the archangel Michael when we say: "May the Lord rebuke you!" And since the foundation of the throne of our Lord is righteousness and justice, He will judge in our favor and against the enemy.

He who works deceit shall not dwell within my house; he who tells lies shall not continue in my presence (Psalms 101:7).

We see that liars and lies cannot stand before the presence of God. For centuries and millennia the accuser has accused people before God. This means that he has to show up with truth.

God is light and in Him everything is like an open book. This is the reason the enemy cannot appear before God with lies, because he would immediately be dismissed.

It is therefore important that we do not discuss whether the accusations that are brought forth against us are right or wrong. When those accusations can be brought before the throne of God it means that there is a reason they can be presented.

It is our job to admit our sins, repent, and ask for forgiveness. Do not react like someone who is offended in their pride and then starts thinking and discussing about it. This would build up barriers on the way into our own freedom. We humble ourselves so that God can lift up our countenance in the presence of our enemies.

I hope that I have been able to explain a few things and clear up some misperceptions in the chapters of this book. I am convinced that in the coming days, weeks, months, and years we will walk in increasing freedom and authority. Rejoice and shout for joy that God will fulfill His plan in your life!

FINAL PRAYER WHEN LEAVING THE COURT OF HEAVEN

Just like it is important to act correctly in a court, it is also important to enter and leave the Courts of Heaven with dignity and by keeping protocol. You may want to do it with a prayer like this:

My heavenly, gracious, and righteous Judge and Father, I thank You for Your grace and for Jesus Christ, Your Son, by whose blood I have been cleansed and through whom my bloodline has been redeemed.

Thank You that You have given me a heart that is ready to repent to thus silence the accuser. I thank You that You have erased my name and any traces, residues, and memories of my bloodline and DNA from contracts, covenant, altars, trading platforms, and any terrestrial or celestial realms and that that You have burnt them up with Your fire. I presented my official repentance and I praise You that the accuser has no more right in these areas. Father, on the foundation of my testimony and of the blood of Jesus Christ You judged all of it. I thank You that the accuser has no more rights to present them before court in the mighty name of Jesus.

My King, as I exit Your courts I give You glory, honor, and praise and I bow myself before You as a confession that You are my King, my Lord, my Judge, my God and Father, You alone.

I love You, my God, Father, Son, and Holy Spirit.

HRVOJE SIROVINA

Hrvoje Sirovina and his wife, Ise, are founders and leaders of the apostolic-prophetic house, *Internationale Gemeinde Esslingen*, a local church in Germany, as well as their international ministry called *HIS Ministries*. Their purpose is to glorify Jesus everywhere they go and to invest into people, empowering them spiritually, activating them socially, and strengthening them economically. With his special teaching gift, Hrvoje releases fresh revelation from the Word of God, which has opened up doors for him to serve in almost forty nations on four continents. Thousands of Bible students, pastors, believers, as well as nonbelievers from all over the globe were released through his apostolic mandate and helped to overcome hindering circumstances, to impact their community, and to change society. Together with their son, Hrvoje and Ise live in the beautiful city of Esslingen in the southwest of Germany.

ROBERT HENDERSON

Robert Henderson is a global apostolic leader who operates in revelation and impartation. His teaching empowers the Body of Christ to see the hidden truths of Scripture clearly and apply them for breakthrough results. Driven by a mandate to disciple nations through writing and speaking, Robert travels extensively around the globe, teaching on the apostolic, the Kingdom of God, the "Seven Mountains," and most notably, the Courts of Heaven. He has been married to Mary for 40 years. They have six children and five grandchildren. Together they are enjoying life in beautiful Midlothian, Texas.